We recently lost our beloved pet "Bear," who was not only our best and dearest friend but also the "Vice President of Sunshine" here at Atlantic Publishing. He did not receive a salary but worked tirelessly 24 hours a day to please his parents. Bear was a rescue dog that turned around and showered me, my wife Sherri, his grandparents Jean, Bob, and Nancy and every person and animal he met (maybe not rabbits) with friendship and love. He made many people smile every day.

We wanted you to know that a portion of the profits of this book will be donated to The Humane Society of the United States. — *Douglas & Sherri Brown*

The human-animal bond is as old as human history. We cherish our animal companions for their unconditional affection and acceptance. We feel a thrill when we glimpse wild creatures in their natural habitat or in our own backyard.

Unfortunately, the human-animal bond at times has been weakened. Humans have exploited some animal species to the point of extinction.

The Humane Society of the United States makes a difference in the lives of animals here at home and worldwide. The HSUS is dedicated to creating a world where our relationship with animals is guided by compassion. We seek a truly humane society in which animals are respected for their intrinsic value and where the human-animal bond is strong.

Want to help animals? We have plenty of suggestions. Adopt a pet from a local shelter, or join The Humane Society and be a part of our work to help companion animals and wildlife. You will be funding our educational, legislative, investigative, and outreach projects in the United States and across the globe.

Or perhaps you'd like to make a memorial donation in honor of a pet, friend, or relative? You can through our Kindred Spirits program. If you'd like to contribute in a more structured way, our Planned Giving Office has suggestions about estate planning, annuities, and even gifts of stock that avoid capital gains taxes.

Maybe you have land that you would like to preserve as a lasting habitat for wildlife. Our Wildlife Land Trust can help you. Perhaps the land you want to share is a backyard—that's enough. Our Urban Wildlife Sanctuary Program will show you how to create a habitat for your wild neighbors.

So you see, it's easy to help animals, and The HSUS is here to help.

THE HUMANE SOCIETY
OF THE UNITED STATES.

2100 L Street NW • Washington, DC 20037 • 202-452-1100

www.hsus.org

Contents

Foreword 6

Introduction...13

Chapter 1: Budgeting and Organization...........................19

Chapter 2: First Things First 37

Chapter 3: Who Does What When? 49

Chapter 4: Location, Location, Location 65

Chapter 5: Attire for the Bride 83

Chapter 6: Attire for the Groom & Wedding Party...........125

Chapter 7: Invitations, Thank You Cards, and More 141

Chapter 8: Wedding Day Flowers 157

Chapter 9: Decorations and Accents 169

How to Plan Your Own Wedding and Save Thousands

Without Going Crazy

By Tracy Leigh

How to Plan Your Own Wedding and Save Thousands—Without Going Crazy

Copyright © 2007 by Atlantic Publishing Group, Inc.
1405 SW 6th Ave. • Ocala, Florida 34471 • 800-814-1132 • 352-622-1875—Fax
Web site: www.atlantic-pub.com • E-mail: sales@atlantic-pub.com
SAN Number: 268-1250

ISBN-13: 978-1-60138-007-4   ISBN-10: 1-60138-007-0

Library of Congress Cataloging-in-Publication Data

Leigh, Tracy, 1969-
  How to plan your own wedding and save thousands : without going crazy / by Tracy Leigh.
     p. cm.
  ISBN-13: 978-1-60138-007-4 (alk. paper)
  ISBN-10: 1-60138-007-0 (alk. paper)
  1. Weddings--Planning. I. Title.

  HQ745.L435 2008
  395.2'2--dc22
                         2007028925

INTERIOR LAYOUT DESIGN: Vickie Taylor • vtaylor@atlantic-pub.com
PROOFREADER: Cathy Bernardy • bernardyjones@gmail.com

Photos courtesy of Xavi Pepe of Petals by Xavi

Printed in the United States

Printed on Recycled Paper

realize that they now need to make cuts in other, potentially vital areas of their wedding plans to stay within budget. This is when it is all too easy to become overwhelmed by the whole experience and begin to feel that you can no longer have the wedding of your dreams because everything costs so much.

My best advice for planning and ultimately having the wedding you both dreamed of is to hire a professional wedding planner and include the planner's fee as part of your overall budget. Aside from keeping you from overspending and overstressing, hiring the right wedding planner will often pay for itself by helping you understand the various services you are buying, educating you as to the appropriate pricing for those services, and often, even helping you negotiate discounts or extras with no additional fees. Working with the best vendors in the industry (and having seen some of the worst) equips every great wedding planner with a level of knowledge and experience that is invaluable to any engaged couple. Moreover, the peace of mind it ends up buying you throughout the whole planning process is priceless.

If you elect to plan your wedding without professional assistance and have already created the budget (and vowed to follow it), then here are some tips, in addition to those included throughout this book, on how to spend your money wisely:

1. Consider that about half of your budget needs to go toward your ceremony location and reception venue, which often includes food and alcohol (assuming you are hosting an open bar).

2. Photography is often the next highest wedding expenditure, and it can be quite costly to hire a quality photographer. Spending over budget on your photography is all too easy to do after you have met a photographer (whom you cannot afford) whose work you end up falling in love with and, despite being out of your budget, you end

up hiring him or her anyway. If this happens, you may be forced to cut significant aspects out of your wedding. To prevent making this mistake, pre-screen photographers on the phone before meeting with them in person to make sure their fees will work with your budget; this will prevent you from wasting their time or yours. However, remember that it is crucial to hire a reputable photographer or risk having poor or no images of this once-in-a-lifetime event you have planned.

3. Flowers and décor should account for at least 20 percent of your overall wedding budget because these are the elements that will set the overall style, mood, and tone of your wedding. The look and feel of your wedding will be what your guests remember for years to come. The flowers, candles, lighting, and overall aesthetic design will provide the dramatic visual that will create the sensational, romantic, or modern setting you have dreamed of.

Naturally, you want your wedding to be visually stunning. The floral aspect of your décor will be one of the first and most important elements you will need to consider. The most popular choices for table centerpieces are tall, round floral arrangements that sit high above the table. Whether on a candelabra or a trumpet vase, the centerpieces alone will be around 50 percent of your entire floral budget. Since these flowers are a significant part of your overall budget, you will want to use them as effectively as possible. So consider using these same arrangements as décor for your ceremony. Simply place your reception table centerpieces on tall, beautiful stands down the aisle, and use your two largest pieces at the altar. If you still have extra centerpieces, place two more at the front of the church or aisle as welcoming arrangements. "Doubling up" your reception flowers at your ceremony will give you a celebrity-style wedding with no additional cost.

4. If you need guidance on where you can trim costs from your budget, consider the area of favors. Allow me to share that, as a wedding

planner, I collect more than 75 percent of the favors at the end of the evening. Although these heartfelt tokens may be sentimental to the bride and groom, I must regretfully say that, in my experience, most of your guests will leave their favors behind or discard them on the way out, even if they are edible. What this tells me is that most people would not mind forgoing the small favors or trinkets but would rather receive a heartfelt note or card instead.

When your budget is not substantial, ingenuity is an asset that you should definitely put to work for you. In what would at first seem like a wedding no-no, cutting the cost of an exorbitant wedding cake is something that can save literally thousands of dollars. I am still astonished that my wedding cake cost $1,200 — and that it was not covered in gold for that price! Several of my brides who have been on extremely tight budgets have asked their mothers or bridesmaids to host a baking event for the bridal party the day before the wedding where they have made a cupcake for each wedding guest. When placed on beautiful silver cupcake tier stands, your cupcakes can have the appearance of a beautiful wedding cake and be an extremely cost-conscious alternative. In addition, memories and photographs of and for the bridesmaids and the soon-to-be mothers-in-law will be priceless.

Engaged couples often find that family members are excited about their impending nuptials as well, and they are always honored to be asked for their help with the big day. For instance, when one of my couples realized that the wedding day transportation costs were excessively high, they asked the bride's cousin to play the part of their wedding day chauffer with his Hummer. He was delighted to be included as part of their wedding party entourage, and the couple ended up paying only for a pre-wedding car detail and a small thank you gift for the cousin's generosity — quite a savings and they still traveled in style.

Your wedding day is a once-in-a-lifetime affair, and there is not a bride or groom who does not want the day to be perfect in every way. When planning a wedding on a budget, countless compromises can be made with little to no effect on your or your guests' enjoyment of the event. Whether you opt to have your invitations made at an offset printer instead of having them engraved, whether you hire a disc jockey instead of a band, or whether you choose a cash bar over an open bar, your goal is to make priority what is important to you. Focus on the aspects of your wedding celebration that will best commemorate this day and ones that you will carry with you into your new future. Most of all, keep things in perspective — whether you serve chicken, fish, or filet mignon at your wedding is not what matters. It is the fact that you and your new spouse will be sharing your first meal together with the friends and family who love you.

By reading this book, you are taking the first step toward creating a budgeted but still beautiful wedding. Here, you will find countless tips to help save you money while at the same time creating the wedding you always dreamed of. Best of luck to you as you begin your journey.

Warmest Wedding Wishes,

Xaviera Pepe

Petals by Xavi
www.petalsbyxavi
www.bestweddingcompany.com
4496 Torrey Pines Dr. Chino Hills Ca 91709
949-307-1918
866-551-2199

Introduction

Becoming engaged is one of the most exciting times in our lives, and you have likely thought about this moment many times. Now you get to plan the wedding of your dreams.

You can picture yourself in your beautiful flowing gown, walking down the aisle toward your handsome groom — all decked out in the finest of tuxes — with your friends and family watching in awe. After the ceremony, you want a reception that includes the best champagne, wonderful music, delectable food, and the pièce de résistance — the perfect wedding cake.

Or perhaps your dreams are to get married on the beach at sunset, in a short, swingy dress, with the waves lapping in the background. Maybe your dream has always been to have the ceremony in your parents' backyard, with a barbecue and pop music for dancing the night away under the stars. It does not matter — whatever your dreams are, they have become the standard for your wedding day.

Whether your vision of a perfect wedding is a small, casual gathering with a limited guest list or a grand formal affair with hundreds in attendance, you want your wedding to be glorious. As the bride, it is your right. This extremely special day should live up to every expectation you have.

With the average cost of a wedding in the United States in 2007 approaching $30,000, you may be stressed about how you are going to afford it. But even with an unlimited budget, wedding planning is not for the weak at heart. There are multitudes of details, from the tiny to the immense, that need to be taken into consideration. When you have to stick to a budget, these details may seem overwhelming. You want the wedding of your dreams, but money is tight.

You must consider your attire and the wedding party's attire, but you will also have to think about the ceremony, flowers, photography, reception, drinks, food, cake, music, and transportation. Those items are just the basics. In addition, you have to worry about all the little extras: centerpieces, memorabilia, Web site, invitations, gifts, tables, chairs, dishes, glasses, place cards. It can be a long list.

The first advice this book offers you is to not become overwhelmed. In this book you will find all the tips and information you need to break down each item into a manageable process. You will learn ways to save money and how to hunt for bargains in every step of the wedding planning process so that you can have the wedding of your dreams, regardless of your budget.

Whether your budget is $1,000 or $50,000, your wedding day dreams can come true.

≈◈ Wedding Facts ◈≈

There are a few facts about weddings that you should know before planning your wedding:

❤ **Face it** — Your wedding is not all about you and your fiancé. Your relatives and friends have opinions about your wedding. Listen courteously, but this is your day; focus on what you want, and do not give into what you do not want.

❤ **Larger than life** — Weddings tend to become twice the size of the original plan. Realizing this to begin with will help you recognize the probability of a bigger guest list than you are anticipating. Chapter 2 covers planning your guest list and how to limit the ever-expanding number of people invited.

❤ **Degrees of perfection** — Although this book shows you how to get the wedding of your dreams on a budget, the perfect, nothing-goes-wrong wedding does not exist. Things happen. Perfectly planned weddings have gone awry because of the unforeseen. The flowers you have your heart set on are not in season or a bridesmaid gains weight and her gown is bursting. Being prepared mentally for the myriad possibilities allows you to focus on the important facets of your wedding: your ceremony and the celebration.

❤ **Money** — The wedding industry is a multibillion dollar competitive market, not a group of sweet, loving individuals who want the best for you. This does not mean that you will not come across incredible people as you plan your wedding, but never forget — their bottom line is the bottom line, and the wedding industry exists to make money.

❤ **Drama** — Weddings elicit strong emotions in everyone involved, and whenever there are strong emotions, drama follows. Whether your bridal party disagrees on their dresses or your great-aunt Matilda insists on bringing her poodle to your formal ceremony, plan on being the mediator to avoid confrontations.

⟪ Your Money, Your Sanity ⟫

Before deciding on your wedding budget, there are some considerations: money and sanity. These guidelines will help you in every step of the wedding planning process; refer to them often as you read this book.

1. **Money can make you crazy.** There will always be a less expensive option. Add in the fact that your wedding costs total will rise until the wedding day is over. Do not stress over the details. Remember, it is supposed to be happy. Stick to your budget, but do not let it overwhelm you.

2. **Money should not be the focus.** When discussing the wedding with your fiancé and family, focus on the beauty of the wedding, the amazing dress you found, or any of the other details. If you focus on money during these conversations, it will quickly override any of the joy you may otherwise feel.

3. **Budgets are important.** Budget for a luxury or two. You will be happier when you do.

4. **Do not be afraid to ask.** Friends and family may know of amazing avenues to save money, but they will expect you to follow their advice.

5. **Accept offers of help.** Whether of time or money, if friends or relatives offer to help, accept it. They will feel good they are helping.

6. **Be brazen for the win.** When negotiating with vendors, you may be able to receive discounts, special pricing, or free add-ons. If you do not ask, you likely will not be offered them. Be brazen and go for the gold.

7. **Start early.** In all areas of your wedding planning, it is essential to take

the time to communicate clearly on your likes, dislikes, budget, and goals. If something is unsatisfactory, do not accept it. Communicate until the situation is resolved to your liking.

8. **Do not be pressured.** Never allow a wedding professional to pressure you into making a purchase. Many professionals receive a commission based on sales, so their pressuring tactics are suspect.

9. **Consider other options.** If you have friends and family in any area of the wedding service industry, consider asking them for a discount or their service at no cost in lieu of a wedding gift.

10. **Special touches at no cost.** Never forget that the most special moments of any wedding are personal touches. Writing your own vows, for example, adds depth and meaning without cost.

11. **Your style is essential.** Instill your personality into your wedding. Your wedding should have a flair that is unique to you and your fiancé. Think about your likes, hobbies, and memories of your time together, and you will be able to personalize your wedding so it is not a cookie-cutter ceremony and reception.

12. **Tradition is nice.** There is no rule that you have to follow tradition. If it is simply something you do not want to do, do not waste money on it.

13. **Stick to your budget.** Allow yourself a few luxuries, but do not go overboard to try to match the extravagance of a friend or family member's wedding. It is too easy to lose track of what is important when your focus changes from having a glorious wedding to keeping up with someone else. Remember your vision, stick to your budget, and you will cherish your day all that much more, because it will be a true reflection of you and your fiancé.

How to Use this Book

You will be guided in:

- ♥ Setting the budget and deciding whether to go formal, informal, or somewhere in between, which will determine the time of day

- ♥ Deciding on the number of guests

- ♥ Setting your wedding date

- ♥ Organizing your plans

- ♥ Selecting the location of your ceremony and reception

Other details such as attire, flowers, and caterers, follow the basics above. This book will present methods for saving money, sticking to your budget, and streamlining the process. You have just hired yourself as your own wedding planner, and this book will give you all the tools you need to be successful. Wedding coordinators plan, advise, supervise, gather information, place orders, delegate, organize, coordinate, and make decisions for their clients' weddings.

It is a massive undertaking — and one you are now handling. This choice alone will save you money, but it is not an easy job. Within this book, you will find the answers you need to know, a guide to help see you through, resources for more information, and sources to find the best deals — in every aspect of the planning of your wedding ceremony and reception.

Chapters 1 through 3 should be read in consecutive order; other chapters can be read as time allows. Enjoy yourself, be happy, and get ready for one of the most amazing experiences of your life: your wedding day.

Budgeting and Organization

This chapter deals with setting your budget and organizational tips and suggestions to be sure to stick to. Having the wedding of your dreams does not depend on having a limitless bank account. The key rests in your budgeting, organizational ability, and follow-through.

Your Wedding Budget

The most important part of planning your wedding is not finding the wedding dress, getting a tremendous deal on your flowers, finagling discounts, or any other single element. Setting your wedding budget takes precedence so that you know how much you can afford for each item.

If your actual "comfortable and reasonably achieved" budget does not seem to be enough for you, resist the temptation to overextend yourself and create a larger budget than you can afford or need. The budget is your key to a happy day.

⊰ Tradition and Who Pays for What ⊱

Wedding expenses used to be easier to figure out. Traditionally, the bride's family pays most of the expenses. Below you will find a chart of who normally pays for what.

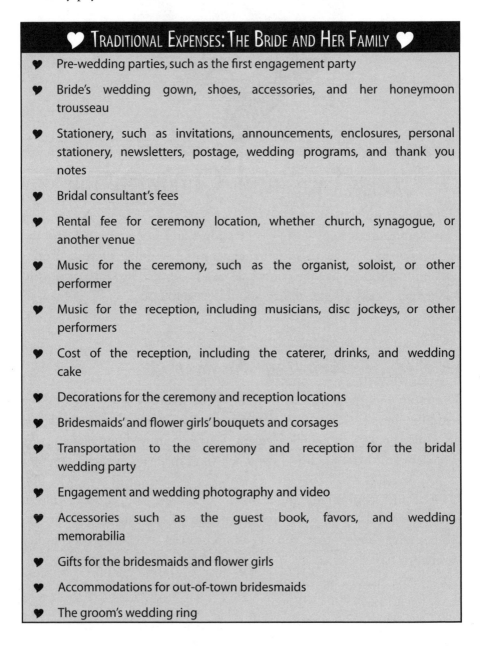

♥ TRADITIONAL EXPENSES: THE BRIDE AND HER FAMILY ♥

♥ Pre-wedding parties, such as the first engagement party

♥ Bride's wedding gown, shoes, accessories, and her honeymoon trousseau

♥ Stationery, such as invitations, announcements, enclosures, personal stationery, newsletters, postage, wedding programs, and thank you notes

♥ Bridal consultant's fees

♥ Rental fee for ceremony location, whether church, synagogue, or another venue

♥ Music for the ceremony, such as the organist, soloist, or other performer

♥ Music for the reception, including musicians, disc jockeys, or other performers

♥ Cost of the reception, including the caterer, drinks, and wedding cake

♥ Decorations for the ceremony and reception locations

♥ Bridesmaids' and flower girls' bouquets and corsages

♥ Transportation to the ceremony and reception for the bridal wedding party

♥ Engagement and wedding photography and video

♥ Accessories such as the guest book, favors, and wedding memorabilia

♥ Gifts for the bridesmaids and flower girls

♥ Accommodations for out-of-town bridesmaids

♥ The groom's wedding ring

❤ TRADITIONAL EXPENSES: THE GROOM AND HIS FAMILY ❤

- ❤ The bride's engagement and wedding rings
- ❤ Groom's attire, shoes, and other accessories
- ❤ Pre-wedding parties, such as a second engagement party, bachelor dinner, and rehearsal dinner
- ❤ Travel and accommodations for family members
- ❤ Accommodations for out-of-town groomsmen
- ❤ Marriage license and fee for the officiant
- ❤ Gifts for the bride, best man, and groomsmen
- ❤ Boutonnieres for the groom, best man, and groomsmen
- ❤ Flowers, including the bride's bouquet and going-away corsage
- ❤ Corsages for the bride's and the groom's mothers and grandmothers
- ❤ Transportation to the airport after the ceremony and reception
- ❤ The honeymoon

❤ TRADITIONAL EXPENSES: MAID OF HONOR AND BRIDESMAIDS ❤

- ❤ Purchase of their dresses, shoes, and accessories
- ❤ Transportation expenses to and from the wedding
- ❤ Wedding gift for the couple, including an individual and a bridal party group gift
- ❤ Showers given by the bridesmaids and the bachelorette party

❤ TRADITIONAL EXPENSES: BEST MAN AND GROOMSMEN ❤

- ❤ Rental of their tuxedos and purchase of their shoes and other accessories
- ❤ Transportation expenses to and from the wedding and personal accommodations if not provided by the groom
- ❤ Wedding gift for the couple, including an individual and a groomsmen's group gift
- ❤ Shared cost of the bachelor party

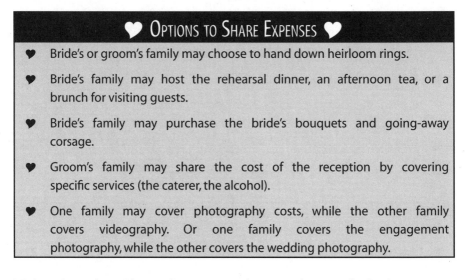

♥ OPTIONS TO SHARE EXPENSES ♥

- ♥ Bride's or groom's family may choose to hand down heirloom rings.

- ♥ Bride's family may host the rehearsal dinner, an afternoon tea, or a brunch for visiting guests.

- ♥ Bride's family may purchase the bride's bouquets and going-away corsage.

- ♥ Groom's family may share the cost of the reception by covering specific services (the caterer, the alcohol).

- ♥ One family may cover photography costs, while the other family covers videography. Or one family covers the engagement photography, while the other covers the wedding photography.

Today, things have changed. More couples contribute to the budget or even assume the entire cost of the wedding. The groom's family is more likely to handle more of the costs than in the past. Whether you are completely in charge of financing your wedding, your family is, your fiancé's family is, or everyone is chipping in, you must first determine the total amount available to spend on your wedding. Then you can make specific plans for each area of the wedding from the total amount available.

When you begin to lay out your budget, consider all sources of money, preferably without taking into account credit cards or borrowing additional funds. Do not start your marriage in debt if you can avoid it.

At this stage it is important to communicate and know what your particular resources are in developing your wedding budget. Find out who is going to pay for what.

Creating Your Wedding Budget

Creating your wedding budget is critical to prevent overspending. Obviously, if you or your families are taking care of everything, making your total budget is simple.

However, in this scenario, let us assume each family, you, and your fiancé are contributing to your wedding budget. Write the actual amount you have to spend. Try to use current and planned savings only, without using credit cards or taking out a loan.

Your next step is to determine how you will break your total budget up to cover each aspect of your wedding. To do this manually, you will want to consider the major areas that encompass a wedding.

Wedding Budget Worksheet

The following worksheet will help you break your total budget into manageable sections:

TOTAL WEDDING BUDGET: $	APPROX. NUMBER OF GUESTS:
Category	**Budget Amount**
Wedding Gown	$
Bridal Accessories	$
Hair, Cosmetics, Spa Treatments	$
Groom's Attire	$
Groom's Accessories	$
Invitations	$
Programs	$
Thank You Cards	$
Ceremony Site	$
Flowers	$
Food/Caterer	$
Alcohol	$
Cake	$
Decorations	$
Music	$
Photography	$
Videography	$
Transportation	$
Wedding Party Gifts	$

TOTAL WEDDING BUDGET: $	APPROX. NUMBER OF GUESTS:
Category	Budget Amount
Memorabilia	$
Misc. Fees (tax, tips, etc.)	$
Officiant's Fees	$

The above worksheet will assist in determining how you are going to spread your budget around, and it is a terrific place to start. But, there is a better way.

Searching for "wedding budget calculators" on any search engine, you can access automatic calculators that will do the work for you. One is **www. outoftheordinary.com/weddingbudgetcalc.php.** This calculator allows you to enter the total dollars you have budgeted, along with the number of guests you plan to invite, and with the click of a button will automatically divvy it up among the various aspects of your wedding. Then you can go through each area and alter the percentage it has pre-assigned if you want to increase it, decrease it, or remove it. Then it will recalculate, according to your specifications.

After you have figured out the dollar amount you will be able to spend on each component of your wedding, you can create an itemized list for the day.

Knowing the dollar amount you are going to spend is critical so that you understand revisions to the budget in case one item turns out to be cheaper or more expensive than you planned, meaning that the amount available for other items changes.

Online Sources

Look at these Web sites for more information on setting your wedding budget:

♥ **http://weddings.about.com/library/blbudgetworksheet.htm**

♥ **http://lifestyle.msn.com/Relationships/CouplesandMarriage/ Articletkt.aspx?cp-documentid=460074**

♥ **http://weddings.about.com/b/a/242437.htm**

♥ **www.usabride.com/wedplan/a_budget.html**

⇒ Start Organized — Stay Organized ⇐

Organization is the next step, after setting your budget, so that you stay within it. If organization is not part of your daily life, this is a good time to begin in preparation for becoming a twosome.

Disorganization will cost time, money, and peace of mind. Start by buying a box of file folders and a file holder. A filing system such as this will keep all those bits of paper from being lost, such as hastily jotted notes, pages from magazines, business cards, and printouts from the computer.

Your Filing System

The best filing systems are often the easiest. Label your file folders and use them to organize all your wedding information. You will be happy you set this up as you begin to acquire increased amounts of wedding paraphernalia.

♥ **Ceremony Location** — Store information here about locations you are considering. After you choose your ceremony location, keep a file on rules, fees, contacts, and any other pertinent information related to the location.

♥ **Ceremony Music** — When you and your fiancé have chosen the music for your ceremony, keep a note of it in this file. You are likely to receive music suggestions from family and friends that can also be filed here for later reference.

♥ **Reception Location** — It can take several visits to many different establishments before deciding on the location for your reception. Each location you visit will have pamphlets, price sheets, and other documentation for your file.

♥ **Reception Music** — When you and your fiancé have chosen music for your reception, keep a note of it in this file. As you interview bands, singers, and disc jockeys, save their information and any specific songs or CDs you want to remember.

♥ **Caterer/Food** — Keep track of menus, pricing lists, and services offered.

♥ **Wedding Cake** — Pictures of cakes you like, bakeries you are interested in, and flavor preferences for you and your fiancé should go in this file. When you choose your bakery and wedding cake, all information should also be filed.

♥ **Stationery** — Invitations, thank-you cards, and program notes should be filed. Catalogs can easily be slipped into the file, as well as samples of paper you particularly like, ideas for designs, verses, and companies you are interested in.

♥ **Flowers** — Make note of your favorite blooms, ideas for your bouquet, decorations, and other florist arrangements in this file. As you see pictures of arrangements that appeal to you, cut them out and save them for reference here. Also, as you visit florists, local and Internet suppliers, list the shop names, the person who assisted you, and your impressions.

♥ **Photographer** — Good photographers are booked far in advance. As you receive recommendations, brochures, advertisements, and other literature on photographers, you will want to file it for reference.

♥ **Wedding Dress** — This is the fun one. As you flip through bridal magazines and see dresses you fall in love with, clip the pictures out and save them. When you purchase your gown, the paperwork should go here, along with a photo of the dress itself — it will help your florist immensely in creating and designing your bouquet. Fitting information can also go here.

♥ **Bridesmaids' Dresses** — Save a picture of the dress your bridesmaids are wearing along with a record of each of their sizes. Swatches of the fabric are also a good idea, again for the florist to use when creating and designing their bouquets. Fitting information can also go here.

♥ **Groom and Groomsmen's Attire** — Clip out photos of tuxedos you and your fiancé are partial to for this file. Rental establishments and fitting information should also be saved.

♥ **Transportation** — If you plan on hiring or renting a specific vehicle for transportation to and from the wedding, the reception, and possibly the airport, keep all related information in this file.

♥ **Memorabilia** — As you search for wedding mementos for yourself and for your guests, clip out pictures, notes of things you especially like, and various vendors.

♥ **Miscellaneous** — If anything in this file begins to take on a greater proportion, create a new file for it.

Other Organizational Tips Checklist

The following tips checklist will give you plenty of organization ideas to use as you approach your special day:

♥ Begin organizing as early as possible to take advantage of savings and to reduce pressure and stress.

♥ Invest in a wedding planner workbook to help you stay on track. Planners are excellent tools with calendars and worksheets for you to have with you for jotting down information.

♥ If you are computer savvy and are more comfortable typing than writing, consider purchasing wedding planning software.

♥ Handheld organizers are amazing tools you can carry with you everywhere you go. Although you cannot store swatches in them, you can store just about everything else — phone numbers, addresses, appointments, to-do lists, and contact lists.

♥ Get absolutely everything in writing. Word of mouth is not a contract; plus, written records will serve as reminders for fees, deadlines, and other information regarding the service or product.

♥ Keep pads of paper anywhere and everywhere you spend time. The car, at work, in the kitchen, on the coffee table so that you will be ready to write something down whenever it occurs to you. As you get busier, you will be grateful for written reminders.

♥ Purchase a small handheld telephone and address book to be used specifically for contacts, addresses, and phone numbers related to your wedding. Find one that is a bright color so it is easy to see, and keep it with you everywhere you go. It will serve as a keepsake after the wedding.

♥ For each service you choose, call the contact throughout the wedding planning months to confirm your order, delivery information, and prices.

♥ Send confirmation letters and keep copies of them for yourself. They will serve as a proof of purchase and as a reminder.

♥ Keep receipts, purchase orders, and any other financial documentation in one place so that you know exactly where to go if you have an issue. Keep these in the filing system described earlier.

♥ Do not pay for anything with cash. Always use either a credit card or a check, so you have a secondary backup of proof of purchase, in case you misplace your receipt.

♥ Never purchase anything if you feel rushed or pressured in any way.

♥ Do not buy the first dress you fall in love with at the first place you see it, unless it is a definite bargain. Write down all applicable information about the item and check around to ascertain you cannot save money on it elsewhere.

❤ Buy a keepsake box or use a shoebox to store samples of fabric, ribbons, lace, pictures of your gown, your ceremony location, and your reception site — and keep it in your car. This way, you will always have the samples you need when you need them.

❤ Create a spreadsheet of all your wedding guests and either print it out or update it on the computer. Beside each name have three columns — Yes, No, and Comments. As you receive your RSVP cards, you will be able to keep track of who is coming and who is not, so you have a current head count.

❤ Send a copy, either by regular mail or e-mail, of the wedding schedule to each member of your wedding party. Keep them apprised of the schedule as it changes so they can keep their calendar clear for important dates.

❤ In addition to the wedding schedule, send out contact lists to each member of the wedding party. Include phone numbers and addresses of all key players in the wedding.

❤ Send e-mails regularly to each member of the wedding party, family, and friends who may be involved in planning to thank them. This is also a good time to update them on any changes, new decisions, or anything else that you want to share.

Online Sources

For more information on organizing your wedding, look at these Web sites:

❤ **www.ultimatewedding.com**

❤ **www.usabride.com/wedplan/a_organize_tips.html**

❤ **www.organizetips.com/wedhelp.htm**

❤ **www.onestopweddingplanner.com**

❧The Wedding Calendar❧

A wedding calendar will be extremely handy for planning. You can use the following calendar, or you can customize it.

As Soon As Possible
Meet with your fiancé's parents as a couple.
Decide on your wedding date and time. (More information on this is in Chapter 2).
Decide on and reserve the locations for the wedding ceremony and the reception. (More information on this is in Chapter 4).
Choose the members of your wedding party. (More information on this is in Chapter 3).
Decide on the formality and the color palette for your wedding.
Set your wedding budget.
Decide how large you want your wedding to be and start your guest list.
Decide how formal you want your reception to be and begin planning it.
Select your wedding gown.
Help your mother and your fiancé's mother with their dress selection.
Meet with your bridesmaids and select their dresses.

Four to Six Months Before the Wedding
Confirm plans for your reception, including decorations, drinks, food, mementos, and entertainment.
Confirm your guest list and double-check with parents for any last-minute invitees.
Select your wedding cake and order it. Be sure your guest list is confirmed before doing this.
Decide if you want to hire a photographer, a videographer, or both. Select who you want to hire, and confirm the arrangements.
Select your florist and decide on a flower plan.
Confirm your music for the ceremony and the reception.
Decide on decorations for your ceremony and your reception.

FOUR TO SIX MONTHS BEFORE THE WEDDING

Talk with friends and family to enlist volunteers to help with the reception, decoration, flowers, music, and any other duties where you require additional support.

Order your invitations or stationery if you are printing them yourself.

THREE MONTHS BEFORE THE WEDDING

Plan the details of your ceremony. This is when you decide on your vows, write them if desired, and confirm any other details, such as music and decorations.

Your fiancé and his best man and groomsmen should reserve their tuxedos.

If the blood tests for your marriage license have not been completed, schedule a medical appointment to have this done.

Enlist volunteers to begin addressing invitations.

TWO MONTHS BEFORE THE WEDDING

Develop a list of poses/shots you and your fiancé want taken by the photographer and/or the videographer.

Select the specific pieces of music you want played and/or performed during your ceremony and reception.

Purchase the small items you will need for your wedding and reception. These may include the basket for the flower girl, the ring pillow for the ring bearer, garter, guest book, and mementos.

Mail the invitations.

You and your fiancé should begin writing thank you notes for any gifts received from engagement parties, showers, and wedding gifts sent to you early.

Decide which items you are renting, rather than purchasing, and arrange for their rental.

ONE MONTH BEFORE THE WEDDING

Speak with your fiancé's parents about the rehearsal dinner and help in any last-minute preparations.

Have your final meetings with vendors, florist, caterer, photographer, videographer, and musician or disc jockey.

Apply for your marriage license.

One Month Before the Wedding

Schedule your final fitting for your wedding gown.

Assist with accommodations for any out-of-town guests who are attending your wedding.

Confirm with your parents that a wedding announcement is being sent to your local paper, or send one yourself.

Plan a luncheon for your maid of honor and bridesmaids.

Three Weeks Before the Wedding

Confirm the wedding rehearsal details and update your wedding party of any changes to the schedule.

Your fiancé should ascertain if his best man has arranged fittings for the tuxedos.

Arrange transportation for the wedding party to and from the ceremony and reception. If someone else is taking care of this, ascertain if it has been done.

Two Weeks Before the Wedding

You and your fiancé should pack for the honeymoon.

Deliver the list of important poses/shots you developed to the photographer and/or the videographer.

Confirm the number of guests who will be attending your reception and notify the caterer.

Develop a seating plan and make place cards for the rehearsal dinner.

Arrange for your wedding gifts to be delivered to your home after the reception. If someone else is responsible for this, ascertain if it is being done.

One Week Before the Wedding

E-mail or mail a schedule of events to all members of your wedding party and any volunteers.

Have your final fitting for your wedding gown.

Confirm with your florist, photographer, videographer, caterer, musician or disc jockey that everything is in order.

Attend a luncheon with your maid of honor and bridesmaids.

Confirm rehearsal plans with the officiant of your ceremony.

ONE WEEK BEFORE THE WEDDING

Pack up supplies for the rehearsal, ceremony, and reception in separate boxes, clearly marking what goes where.

The days before your wedding should be organized, with lists of chores that need to be done, who is doing each one, and an up-to-the-moment wedding calendar, so that you will handle deadlines with grace.

≈ Final Thoughts ≈

If setting a budget and being organized annoy you, remind yourself of your goal — to have a wonderful wedding, your way, while saving money.

It is feasible, but it takes more than searching the best bargains locally or on the Internet. Determine your wedding budget, who is contributing to it, and how you are dividing it among expenses. Overspending happens when people are not prepared, do not plan ahead, and do not realize how much money they have to spend.

Second, it is important to organize the planning process to keep track of progress. Organization will give you the tools you need to grab a receipt, a contract, a picture, or anything else you need the minute you need it. Organization allows you to be in control. When combined, budgeting and organization will give you a massive head start in achieving the wedding you want, for the price you want, without becoming overwhelmed.

Budgeting and planning are worth the time; you are worth it, and the celebration of your marriage is worth it.

Case Study: KL Wedding Designs, LLC

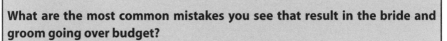

What is your area of expertise?

I am a wedding consultant, and I assist couples in planning their wedding. Whether they would like me to be involved in the entire planning process or they just need help selecting vendors, I offer a variety of planning packages to fit any couples' needs.

What are the most common mistakes you see that result in the bride and groom going over budget?

One of the most common mistakes is not establishing an initial budget. This does not mean just deciding how much money you are going to spend on the wedding, but also establishing what percent of your budget you want to spend in each area of the wedding. As a wedding consultant, one of my jobs is to keep track of a couple's wedding budget to make sure they stick to it.

If you could offer one piece of advice to a couple planning their own wedding under a budget, what would it be?

The advice I would offer to a couple planning their own wedding is to not just decide how much money to spend on the wedding but to also decide how much money to spend on each part of their wedding. For example, 11 percent of the budget usually goes to bridal attire, 8 percent to photography, 6 percent to flowers, and 40 percent to reception and so on.

What are overlooked areas of savings?

The wedding reception is the most often overlooked area of savings in the wedding industry. The wedding reception is usually the largest total cost of the wedding (40 percent of the budget) so it is also the place where you may be able to save the most. Be sure to sit down with your contact at the reception venue to discuss different food and bar options to keep your costs down. For example, maybe have stations of heavy hors d'oeuvres set up in place of a buffet or even sit-down dinner. Create a signature drink to be served in place of a full-service bar, or serve only wine with your dinner.

A second area of savings would be with the stationery. Computers have made it very easy for couples to create their own invitations, save-the-date cards, menu cards, programs, etc. By creating their own, couples can cut down on the extra costs of calligraphy and printing fees.

How do a bride and groom stay within their budget?

Establish a well-planned budget and determine how much money will be spent

CASE STUDY: KL WEDDING DESIGNS, LLC

in each area — if you do go over budget in one area, make sure you are prepared to make sacrifices in another area.

What is the biggest misconception you see in wedding planning?

The biggest misconception today is that hiring a wedding consultant is viewed as an extra expense. The truth is just the opposite; consultants are great resources for cost-cutting tips and can usually get additional discounts from your vendors. Also, a consultant is your best resource to keep you on budget because part of their job description is to keep an eye on your budget to make sure you don't go over.

How can a couple find quality services at the best price?

A couple should not be afraid to shop around. Even if they think a vendor is out of their price range, they may be surprised by some of the less expensive packages they offer. Also, don't be afraid to ask your vendors if they are running any promotions or if they are willing to give you any additional discounts — most couples would be surprised to see how flexible some vendors are.

What shouldn't the bride and groom do to cut costs?

A bride and groom should never hire a friend or family member to act as one of their vendors. For example, many couples think that just because their Aunt Sally takes good pictures that she would be a good photographer for the wedding — not the case. <u>Always</u> hire a professional.

Do you have an example to share that shows how a bride and groom saved money?

- ♥ One couple hired a professional videographer for their wedding but then had a student at a local university do all the editing.

- ♥ Another couple found that it was cheaper to buy their own vases for their centerpieces instead of renting from the florist.

- ♥ A Friday wedding is always less expensive than a Saturday wedding.

It's easy to become overwhelmed when planning a wedding. What is your advice for lowering their stress?

My advice for lowering stress would be to hire a wedding consultant. The main reason I got into this business is because I know how stressful planning a wedding can be, but it is also supposed to be one of the happiest days of your life. Having

Case Study: KL Wedding Designs, LLC

a professional on your side to make sure everything is going smoothly is the best decision a couple can make.

How would a couple know when a price is truly "too good to be true"?

I don't believe that there is such a thing as a price that is "too good to be true" — most couples would be surprised by the variety of packages vendors offer to fit any couple's budget. However, if a couple has concerns about the price, I would suggest that they ask the vendor for references, and if the vendor is unable to provide those, then the couple should definitely go with another company.

Any other suggestions or advice you would like to share?

I would advise couples to read all contracts very carefully; oftentimes there are hidden costs within the contracts. For example, in addition to your fee for your photographer, you may also be required to purchase a wedding album, or your reception hall may charge a napkin-folding fee.

Kerry Leedy

190 N. Glen Oak Drive

Springboro, OH 45066

513-560-1110

www.klweddingdesigns.com

KL Wedding Designs LLC

First Things First

It is impossible to hire a caterer if you do not know how many guests are attending. Purchasing your wedding gown must be postponed until you have decided whether your wedding will be formal or informal. If you have not set a date yet, you will want to know if certain seasons offer you built-in savings. This chapter focuses on the order of these decisions and offers information to help you feel confident when you make them.

Determining Your Wedding Vision

As the bride, you already have a vision of how you want your wedding. Your fiancé may have another vision, one distinctly different than yours. It is time to discuss each of your visions so you can meld them into one. This will be the basis for every area of the wedding planning process, so it is important to take the time needed to agree.

Your Wedding Vision Worksheet

Use this worksheet to determine the vision for your wedding.

Check all that apply:

WEDDING DESCRIPTION		LOCALE	
	Formal		Your Home
	Informal		Bride's Hometown
	Traditional		Groom's Hometown
	Nontraditional		Other Location
	Casual		Indoor Ceremony
	Festive		Outdoor Ceremony
	Religious		Church — Religious
	Contemporary		Other — Non-Religious

WEDDING DESCRIPTION		SEASON	
	Intimate (less than 50)		Spring
	Small (51 to 125)		Summer
	Medium (126 to 250)		Autumn
	Large (more than 251)		Winter

HOUR OF THE DAY		COLOR PALETTE	
	Sunrise		Pastels
	Midday		Rich Hues (Jewel Tones)
	Sunset		All White
	Evening		Black and White
	Late Night		Bright Hues (Primary Colors)

BRIDE'S PRIORITIES		GROOM'S PRIORITIES	
	Season		Season
	Location		Location
	Guest List		Guest List
	Type of Ceremony		Type of Ceremony
	Reception Location		Reception Location
	Decorations		Decorations
	Food and Drink		Food and Drink
	Entertainment		Entertainment
	Attire		Attire

BRIDE'S PRIORITIES		GROOM'S PRIORITIES	
	Memorabilia		Memorabilia
	Other:		Other:

Ideally, after going through the worksheet, you will have a clearer focus on the overall picture of your wedding and will be that much closer to merging your visions into one.

❧ *Your Wedding Guest List* ❧

There are many reasons why determining your guest list should take priority at this stage. Your choice of venue for the ceremony and the reception may differ depending on the size of your wedding. A formal ceremony is unlikely to be held outdoors, while a casual ceremony is unlikely to be held in a grand church or synagogue. Because of this, your guest list is one of the most important elements in your wedding. Guest lists grow, and you may have to be diligent to keep the numbers in your budgeted range.

When compiling your guest list, consider having fewer guests to allow you and your fiancé to extend your budget since the guest list has a domino effect on nearly all areas of the wedding. If you and your fiancé are paying for the wedding in full, you decide who to invite. If your parents are financing all or a portion of the wedding costs, they will also have a say in who is invited. If there are any arguments over certain guests, you and your fiancé should have the final say.

Guest lists for weddings normally include these groups of people:

- ♥ Parents and Stepparents
- ♥ Bride's and Groom's Children
- ♥ Siblings, Step-Siblings, and Best Friends
- ♥ Grandparents and Step-Grandparents
- ♥ Aunts, Uncles, Nieces, and Nephews

- ♥ Close Friends and First Cousins

- ♥ Business Associates and Dignitaries

- ♥ Second Cousins and Acquaintances

After you know how large your wedding is going to be, divide the maximum number of guests up between you, your fiancé, your parents, and his parents. Each of these groups should do the following:

1. Prepare a list of the "must-have" individuals. These are the people who each of you feel absolutely must be invited.

2. Prepare a list of the "not allowed" individuals. These are the people who each of you feel absolutely must not be invited.

3. Prepare a list of those that "should be" invited but you believe will not attend because of their location, comfort levels, or any other criteria that would put them on this list.

4. Prepare a list of individuals you would like to invite if there is room. This group includes casual friends, colleagues, distant family relations, and others who do not fit in the above three lists.

5. Add them all up. If the total is within your budget, all is well and you can confirm your wedding guest list.

6. If the total exceeds your predetermined wedding size, it is time to start trimming the guest list. Consider the following when trimming the guest list:

   - ♥ Dates of single guests

   - ♥ Children

   - ♥ Those neither of you have spoken to in more than a year

   - ♥ Those who would feel obligated to come if invited but whose feelings would not be hurt if they were not

❤ Consider cutting an entire group, such as all work colleagues, club members, or other groups

❤ Those neither you nor your fiancé personally know, such as individuals associated with your parents.

❤ If still over your limit, rank the guest list in order of importance and cut from the bottom up, until the number of guests equals the determined size of your wedding.

Do not be afraid to be ruthless when trimming your guest list. It will affect the cost of nearly everything in your wedding. You will almost certainly go over budget if you are over your planned limit. The difference between 100 guests and 150 guests is significant in terms of the final cost of the caterer, restaurants, banquet halls, liquor served, and the wedding cake.

Tempers can flare at this stage of planning your wedding, but be firm in your resolve. If anyone insists on someone's being invited but is over an allotted number of invitees, someone else will not be invited. The bottom line does not move.

Wedding Guest Worksheet

Below is a worksheet to help you get started in developing your guest list. It is simple in concept but will show you the numbers in a concise format. Attendant information is also included:

PRE-DETERMINED NUMBER OF GUESTS	ACTUAL NUMBER OF GUESTS:
Bride:	Bride:
Groom:	Groom:
Bride's Parents:	Bride's Parents:
Groom's Parents:	Groom's Parents:
Number of Attendants:	Number of Attendants:
Number Over:	Number Trimmed:
Final Guest List Tally:	

There are also some terrific online sources for guest planning. The Wedding Channel.com has a Guest List Manager, **www.weddingchannel.com/tools. html**, which can be accessed by registering at the site. Registration is free.

Online Sources

For more information on planning your guest list, the following Web sites may be of interest to you:

♥   **http://weddings.about.com/od/getorganized/a/StartGuestList.htm**

♥   **http://ourmarriage.com/planner/html/wedding_guest_list.html**

Formal, Semiformal, or Informal

Your wedding day is a reflection of you and your fiancé, your marriage, and your individual and combined styles. Whether you choose to have a formal, semiformal, or an informal wedding is one of the decisions you will have to make.

You may have already decided on the type of wedding you want to have, but if you have not, the following information may help.

The Formal Wedding

A formal wedding is the most expensive. It can be held in any locale. The details in a formal wedding, as opposed to a semiformal or an informal wedding, lie in the attire of the wedding party, the elegance of the reception, and even in the size of the guest list.

In a formal wedding, the atmosphere tends to be solemn and reserved, with at least four attendants. Attire is flashier, with the groom and groomsmen wearing tailcoats and the bride and bridal party in long gowns. If you choose a formal wedding, you will need to stipulate a dress code on your invitations for the guests, as they should be in more elegant attire. Your guest list will likely be medium to large, but small weddings can also be formal.

Dinner is a formal sit-down meal with several courses being served. Transportation is also fancier, with the bride and groom arriving at the ceremony and reception in a limousine or horse-drawn carriage. Entertainment at a formal wedding will likely be provided by an orchestra or band.

Decorations will be in abundance, with the fragrance of exotic fresh flowers filling the air. Mementos and memorabilia cost more, such as bottles of wine or engraved silver keepsakes.

If you have your heart set on a fairy tale wedding, you are likely envisioning a formal wedding.

The Semiformal Wedding

A semiformal wedding is an excellent choice for those desiring a formal wedding with less rigidity and more freedom in attire, food, and decorating. A bride does not have as many attendants and her bridal party's gowns are less formal, though the bride can have a formal gown if she chooses. The groom and groomsmen may decide to wear a suit instead of formal tuxedos, or if they do choose to wear tuxes, they are likely not tailcoats. The guests do not have to dress so formally, though they are expected to dress nicely.

A band or a disc jockey provides music. Instead of a sit-down meal, semiformal weddings have a buffet-style course. If the meal is a sit-down one, it will have fewer courses.

Decorations likely have fewer flowers than a formal wedding, but semiformal weddings make up for it in other ways. Candles, balloons, and banners are popular. Memorabilia will be less costly than that of a formal wedding.

If you are not up for the rigidity of a formal wedding but want something more elegant than an informal wedding, a semiformal wedding may be perfect for you.

The Informal Wedding

An informal wedding is the most casual of the three and can take place at a beach, in a backyard ceremony, or in a chapel. The bride may choose to have one to three attendants, and the attire is as casual as the bride and groom deem to be appropriate. For indoor weddings, a tea-length to a floor-length dress will be worn by the bride and her bridal party. For outdoor weddings, attire will largely depend on the venue.

Entertainment will be a disc jockey or a friend playing CDs as a favor to the couple, though a band is also appropriate. Decorations are likely to be scaled down to a minimum of flowers but possibly with more balloons, banners, and streamers. The wedding meal is almost certain to be a buffet style or, for outdoor receptions, a barbeque. For an informal wedding, hors d'oeuvres and cocktails may be served instead of a full meal, along with the wedding cake.

If you and your fiancé are looking for a laid-back, relaxed, and comfortable atmosphere for your wedding, the informal wedding will deliver.

Of course, none of the above is set in stone. Choose what you want, and be prepared to plan. Be sure you spend your wedding day your way.

Online Sources

For more information on styles of weddings, the following Web sites may be of interest to you:

♥   **www.easyweddings.com.au/information/wedding_styles.asp**

♥   **http://weddings.about.com/cs/bridesandgrooms/a/weddingstyle.htm**

Setting Your Wedding Date

Before you can choose the locale for your wedding ceremony and your reception, you have to know the date and the time. You will be able to take advantage of increased savings the sooner you begin to plan your wedding because you will not feel rushed to commit to a site too quickly and you can comparison shop. Ideally, four to six months is the average time to plan a wedding. More time affords you more choices, flexibility, and availability of venues.

The Wedding Season

The timing of your wedding could cost you more or less money. Busier wedding seasons mean everything is more expensive; less busy wedding seasons offer a better value for your money. The most popular months for weddings are June, August, and September, with May, July, October, and December next in popularity. These months will show increased fees, less availability, and more frustration for you and your fiancé.

Vendors have emptier calendars during "off" months and are more likely to offer less pricey fees. Also, if there is a location you like but it is booked when you wanted to have your wedding, you may be able to snatch it up at an incredible rate during an off month.

Other expensive times to consider are any holidays throughout the year. Valentine's Day wedding ceremonies may be romantic, but they cost more money. Reconsider setting your wedding date the week of Valentine's Day.

It is important to compare prices for any date you set. Choose three separate wedding dates and shop for the one that costs the least.

The Wedding Day

It is unlikely you will want to be married on a Wednesday, but Saturday is the busiest, most expensive day for a wedding. If you are considering a significantly small wedding, a weekday or a Sunday ceremony may be worth checking out. Some bridal businesses even offer nontraditional wedding day discounts.

If your wedding must be on a Saturday, there are other ways to find savings, but talk over the idea of a Friday evening or Sunday morning/afternoon ceremony with your fiancé and your family. If you go this route, you will most assuredly save money and open your budget up in other areas. Plus, availability will be easier. If you do not have time to plan your wedding, this is an option for you.

The Wedding Time

The time of your wedding is essential to your wedding budget and to the style of your ceremony. Take the following tips into consideration when deciding your wedding time:

♥ Wedding services and sites charge rates depending on the time of day of your wedding. Because of this, you may find it less expensive to be married in the morning rather than the afternoon or evening. As you consider different locales, do not forget to ask if there is a time factor in relation to their fees. If, for example, you are having a late-night wedding, you may be charged extra for cleanup if the staff has to arrive the following morning to begin. This could equal a full extra day rental fee. Pay close attention, and ask whenever you are unsure about any potential charges.

♥ The time of your wedding and reception reflects the formality of your wedding. Tradition dictates that a morning ceremony, with possibly a brunch reception, will cost far less than an elegantly formal candlelit ceremony with a catered five-course sit-down dinner reception. You and your fiancé should discuss what type of reception you both want, and use that as a guide to choosing your ceremony time.

♥ An early afternoon wedding can also save you money. Instead of having a full dinner reception, you could have an afternoon tea or a selection of hors d'oeuvres. Both of these suggestions can be presented in an extremely elegant manner. Food tops the list for cost, so if your budget is especially tight, this is one way to shave a considerable amount off your bottom line.

♥ In addition to food, alcohol is a budget-breaker for many couples planning their wedding. A late-morning or early afternoon wedding will allow you to serve only nonalcoholic beverages.

❤ If your heart is set on having your wedding outside, a late morning or early evening wedding will offer milder temperatures in the summer. You can see a listing of typical weather, based on location, here: **www.weather.com/activities/events/weddings/setthedate/index.html?from=wed_welcome**.

❤ Depending on the locality of your wedding and reception, certain times of day may mean heavier traffic affecting the arrival times for your guests, the officiant, and your cake, as well as you and your fiancé.

❤ Consider your guests' schedules when setting the time for your wedding. If you decide on a Friday evening ceremony, you may want to push the start time to 7 p.m., rather than 6, so that people coming from work have time to go home before arriving at the ceremony location.

❤ Another benefit to having an earlier ceremony and reception is greater flexibility for you and your fiancé. You will be able to leave for your honeymoon the same day as your wedding, rather than waiting until the following morning.

Other Considerations on Setting Your Wedding Date

In setting your wedding date, there are two main approaches:

1. You can choose the date and then locate sites and services that are available. This is the more traditional option.

2. You can narrow down a season and a month and then set your wedding date based on the availability of the ceremony and reception site.

Number two allows you to choose the services and locales you most want by being flexible with your exact wedding date. Another option is to merge numbers one and two by selecting three or four potential wedding dates and then researching those to see which date delivers the most savings and availability of your wanted locales and services.

Do not forget the following:

- ♥ Possible vacations of family and friends that may coincide with your wedding date.

- ♥ Any special dates that either you or your fiancé would like to commemorate by having your ceremony on that day.

- ♥ If you have a definite location in mind for the ceremony and the reception, are they both available for the date(s) you have in mind?

- ♥ Out-of-town guests who need accommodations while in town. If you live near a college, for example, make sure your date is not the weekend of graduation, when most hotels are booked.

- ♥ How much time it will take you to plan your wedding. If you require more time to make decisions, know this when you set your wedding date, and plan accordingly.

- ♥ If you have your heart set on an outdoor wedding, think about the weather where the wedding will take place.

⟫Final Thoughts⟪

Setting your wedding date should be fun — not stressful. If you and your fiancé have different ideas for the date, find some middle ground. Communicate with each other, discover what is most important to each of you, and compromise if necessary.

Who Does What When?

Ideally, the wedding party you and your fiancé select will assist in various duties. Understanding traditional wedding party etiquette is essential. Before deciding on attendants, understand who is supposed to do what, and communicate the duties to each person.

Traditional Wedding Party Etiquette

The Maid of Honor

Other than the bride and the groom, the maid (or matron) of honor is one of the most critical roles. Before the wedding, she will go with you to shop for your dress and other accessories; she can help you address invitations, organize your bridal shower, and record wedding gifts as they arrive. During the ceremony and reception, she will distribute the corsages and boutonnieres; assist you with your dress, makeup, and hair; and assist the bridesmaids with their preparation. She can hold your bouquet and your fiancé's ring, serve as an official witness to the vows, arrange your train and veil, and keep wedding attire during the honeymoon.

The Best Man

Flexibility is one trait to consider when deciding who should be the best man. Before the wedding, he will encourage your fiancé when stressed, make travel arrangements for you and your fiancé, ascertain if all fittings are completed by the groomsmen, and organize your fiancé's bachelor party. During the wedding ceremony and reception, he oversees the ushers, acts as an official witness to the vows, holds your ring, safeguards the marriage license, pays the honorarium fee to the officiant, and proposes a toast at the bridal table. After the wedding, he will return all the rented tuxedos.

The Bridesmaids

Your bridesmaids can assist in making wedding favors and mementos, run errands for you, assist in addressing invitations, and assist the maid of honor with your bridal shower and bachelorette party. During the wedding ceremony and reception, they can help in small ways on an as-needed basis. Also, they should feel comfortable being with your guests and dancing with the groomsmen.

The Groomsmen

The groomsmen are the first people your guests see when they arrive at your ceremony location. Their responsibilities include arranging transportation for your bridesmaids to the ceremony, greeting guests and ushering them to their seats, seating your mother and your fiancé's mother just before the ceremony, escorting them back down the aisle afterward, assisting your mother with any last-minute details, mingling with your guests at the reception, and dancing with your bridesmaids.

If you and your fiancé decide to choose separate attendants as ushers, they are responsible for greeting and seating your guests, your mother, and your fiancé's mother.

The Flower Girls

If there are one, two, or more special little girls in your life, you may decide to have flower girls. Their only responsibility is during the ceremony when they walk down the aisle sprinkling flower petals on the ground to signify your entrance. If you would like to give them additional duties, things such as helping with the gift table, the guest registry, and handing out favors are all possibilities.

The Ring Bearer

If you or your fiancé have a young boy who is special to you, you may decide to include him as the ring bearer. He carries a pillow with the wedding rings of the bride and groom sewn on it. Many couples decide to have the flower girl and the ring bearer walk side by side.

Wedding Party Responsibility Chart

The following chart will give you a quick overview of traditional wedding party responsibilities.

THE MAID OF HONOR	THE BEST MAN
Assists the bride with pre-wedding plans, such as scouting locations, seating plans, registering	Is in charge of overseeing and making arrangements for the bachelor party
Assists the bride in selecting her wedding gown and the bridesmaids' gowns	Sets up time to get fitted for his personal tuxedo
Purchases own gown and arranges for personal fitting of gown.	Ascertains if the groomsmen have been measured for their tuxes
Often assists in addressing the wedding invitations	Is in attendance at the wedding rehearsal and at the rehearsal dinner.
Plans a bridal shower for the bride	Provides transportation, either by driving or hiring a driver, for the groom to the wedding ceremony
Is in attendance at the wedding rehearsal and at the rehearsal dinner.	Brings any boxes or gifts to the ceremony and reception
Ascertains if the bridesmaids are in place at their appropriate locations before the ceremony	Helps the groom dress

THE MAID OF HONOR	THE BEST MAN
Assists the bride with makeup, hair, and dressing before the ceremony	Gives the honorarium fee to the officiant
Holds the bride's bouquet and the groom's wedding ring at the altar during the ceremony	Holds the bride's ring during the ceremony
Signs the wedding certificate	Signs the wedding certificate
If requested, stands in the receiving line with the bride, groom, and parents	Offers the first toast to the wedding couple at the reception
May offer a toast to the wedding couple at the reception	Arranges transportation or drives the bride and groom to the airport or the hotel after the reception
Assists the bride in any changes of clothing, such as a reception gown or a going-away outfit	Returns all the tuxedos to the rental facility after the reception
Helps the best man deliver gifts to the bride and groom's residence after the reception	Helps the maid of honor deliver gifts to the bride and groom's residence after the reception

THE BRIDESMAIDS	THE GROOMSMEN
Help in pre-planning, such as assisting in addressing the invitations	Help plan and attend the groom's bachelor party
Participate in the planning and carrying off of the bridal shower	Arrange fittings and pay for renting personal tuxedo
Purchase own gowns and arrange for personal fittings of gown	Escort guests to their seats at the ceremony
Are in attendance at the wedding rehearsal and at the rehearsal dinner	Escort the mother of the bride and mother of the groom to their seats at the ceremony
Circulate during the reception, talking and dancing with guests and groomsmen	Circulate during the reception, talking and dancing with guests and the bridesmaids

In addition, the wedding party helps in planning the wedding, placing the decorations at the wedding and the ceremony, and transporting out-of-town guests from the airport and to the ceremony from their hotel. Other duties may be bestowed on the wedding party members, as long as they are willing to step in and lend a helping hand.

Online Sources

For more information on wedding etiquette, the following Web sites may be of interest to you:

- ❤ **www.topweddinglinks.com/etiquette.html**

- ❤ **http://ourmarriage.com/html/wedding_etiquette.html**

- ❤ **www.superweddings.com/etiquette.html**

Selecting Your Attendants

You will need to decide how large you want your wedding party, and whom you select is important. Although there are traditional and other "rules" to help guide you, the end choice is completely yours. Consider the following:

- ❤ How large is your wedding? One attendant per 50 invited guests is a traditional method to decide the size of your wedding party.

- ❤ Formality. For an extremely formal ceremony, four or more is an appropriate number. Semiformal weddings tend to have at least three attendants, and informal ceremonies rarely have more than three.

- ❤ Just because someone lives far away does not mean he or she would not be interested in being in your wedding party. Do not assume you will be turned down. Ask; you may be pleasantly surprised.

- ❤ Symmetry is not important. If your fiancé has only two friends or family members he is interested in asking to be in your wedding party but you have four, it is fine. No one will care.

- ❤ Children are not absolutely necessary. Flower girls and ring bearers are completely optional and are not in many wedding ceremonies.

The end decision is completely up to you and your fiancé. If you wish to have two attendants at a formal wedding, do so. If you are having an informal ceremony but would like to have a large wedding party, go for it. When you have decided how many people you want to have in your wedding party, the next step is to choose those you would like to ask.

You and your fiancé will want to determine who the special people in your lives are. When you have your list of names, consider who should be your maid of honor and who should be your fiancé's best man. These are two critical spots to fill. They will help in the planning of the wedding and have roles in the ceremony and reception.

When you have your list of names and you are ready to ask, these pointers will help you:

♥ Do not wait too long to invite your chosen attendants. For one, you do not want to be the cause of hurt feelings; second, you need to know as soon as possible if they are going to say yes or no.

♥ Do not assume that each of your attendants knows what his or her duties are going to be. Give each individual a list of what you consider the responsibilities to be so that each is aware from day one.

♥ Remember that your wedding party members have their own lives and responsibilities. They may need advanced warning.

♥ Remember to communicate regularly with your wedding party. One suggestion is to use e-mail so everyone can correspond easily.

Additional Budget Considerations in Selecting Your Wedding Party

Before bestowing the honors on any of your friends and family, there are some cost-cutting tips:

1. Smaller wedding parties equal savings. If you have a large wedding

party, you will have that many more gifts to purchase. If you are paying for accommodations for out-of-town attendants, the more you have, the more you pay. Each attendant can equal upward of $200 out of your budget.

2. Consider having only a maid of honor and a best man without any bridesmaids or groomsmen to save on costs. Male relatives or friends can act as ushers.

3. If you know several young girls, consider having only flower girls. Your wedding would be unique, and the wedding processional would be adorable.

4. When choosing your attendants, especially your maid of honor and best man, pick responsible individuals who will truly help. You will save time, which is worth money, if you have people on your side that will be happy to help out. If your attendants are irresponsible, you will likely waste a good deal of your precious time ascertaining that things are getting accomplished.

5. Choose attendants who communicate well with you. An essential component of saving money is organization. You will need to be able to communicate schedule updates and changes with your wedding party, and poor communication is costly.

6. Do not offer to reimburse your attendants for their attire or travel. Although this is a grand gesture and sure to be appreciated, you do not have an endless budget.

7. Consider their budgets as well as yours. If your maid of honor has the ability to spend a large amount on her gown, but the bridesmaids you choose do not, there are sure to be recriminations.

Beyond the Traditional — Other Attendant Possibilities

If you are worried about hurting someone's feelings because you want a small wedding party but have a large group of friends and family to choose from, your best bet is honesty. Talk to those you have not asked to be attendants and explain that your preference is for a smaller wedding party. You could also plan specific jobs and projects for other friends and family members to handle.

There are plenty of ways for everyone you care about to be an important part of your wedding. Some of them will even save you money. Consider these ideas:

♥ **Invitations** — Have someone address, stamp, and deliver them to the post office.

♥ **Out-of-Town Contact** — Ask someone to take care of keeping out-of-town guests informed of any changes, providing maps of the wedding locality, securing hotel accommodations, providing transportation from the airport to the hotel, the hotel to the ceremony, and doing anything else that will assist your far-away guests to feel more comfortable.

♥ **Program Distributors** — If you do not have ushers, have a friend hand out the programs. Position the person (or child) by the door to hand out programs as guests arrive.

♥ **Candle Lighters** — Assign two people the job of lighting the candles at the altar and the ones at the pews. It is an important job, and the ambience of the ceremony will change as they are being lit, one by one.

♥ **Soloists** — If you have a friend or family member who sings well, ask the person to sing at your ceremony.

♥ **Readers** — Ask someone special to read either poetry or scripture during your ceremony.

♥ **Guest Book Attendant(s)** — This job can easily be divided among several people. Ask them to stand near your guest book and greet guests as they arrive to your ceremony and your reception.

♥ **Rose Petals/Bird Seed/Confetti/Rice** — Whatever you choose, you can ask people to assist in several different ways. They can help create the containers and hand them out to guests as they leave the ceremony, so that when you and your groom run out, everyone will be ready to cheer.

♥ **Reception Ushers** — If your reception has assigned seating, ask several friends and/or family members to meet guests as they arrive and show them to their seats.

♥ **Gift Table** — This is a great job for children, but anyone can do it. Just ask them to stand near the reception entrance to guide guests to the gift table. Alternately, they can accept the gift from your guests and place them on the table. Have some tape on hand so they can also tape the card to the gift. This will make certain you have the present and the card when you open it.

♥ **Favors/Mementos** — This is another role for children, but it can be done by anyone. Ask several people to walk around the reception handing out favors and mementos to the guests.

In addition, there is one role you and your fiancé should seriously consider filling. You will need people to be your eyes and ears and to follow up on potential issues at your ceremony and reception.

You and your fiancé will have spent months preparing for your wedding. Now that it is here, you should be able to enjoy it without worrying about the details. Those in your wedding party will also be busy attending to their various duties. Plus, the entire wedding party and your family will be required to pose for photos. Therefore, you should consider asking two or more people to be in charge of the last-minute details and the actual choreography of your wedding ceremony and reception. Anyone who is good at organization, planning, and thinking on their feet would be an excellent candidate for this job.

Tasks may include:

♥ Checking on various details before and after the ceremony and during the reception

♥ Finding missing members of the wedding party when it is time for pictures to be taken

♥ Being the "go-to" people for caterers, entertainers, and any other service professionals

♥ Reminding the best man he will be giving a toast at the reception. Ask the maid of honor if she also wants to toast the happy couple.

♥ Ascertaining that transportation for the wedding party is taken care of for after the ceremony and for the bride and groom for after the reception

The friends and family members you pick to be in your wedding party and those who agree to step in and help in other ways will be critical from the day they agree to help. Because these roles are so important, take the time you and your fiancé need to agree on whom to ask and how to divvy up the responsibilities. Your wedding will be much more special because of them.

Parents of the Bride and Groom

You and your fiancé's parents are also a part of your wedding party, simply by virtue of being your parents. Traditionally, the bride's parents have more responsibilities than the groom's, but weddings today are changing. If your fiancé wants his parents to play a greater role in the planning of your wedding and in the ceremony and if they also would like to, many of the wedding responsibilities can be passed on to them.

The Bride's Mother

Your mother's main function in your wedding is to help you plan according to your tastes and style. If you prefer to hand the reigns over to Mom, you certainly can, but most brides prefer to guide their wedding their way. You and your mother may want to take some time to go over the following list of responsibilities and personalize it for your wedding and your wishes.

Before the Wedding, the Mother of the Bride

1. Traditionally hosts the first engagement party.

2. Customarily contributes financially to the wedding budget.

3. Assists you and your fiancé in choosing the venue for your wedding ceremony and for the reception.

4. Assists you in developing your family's guest list for the ceremony.

5. Discusses various possibilities for different types of ceremonies with you, including family or traditional customs.

6. May help you shop for and choose your wedding gown and other accessories.

7. Chooses her dress for the ceremony. She may coordinate formality and color with the mother of the groom.

8. Plans and hosts a bridal shower, either along with the maid of honor or a secondary shower.

9. Assists you in your preparations before the ceremony, including your dress, cosmetics, hair, and anything else you may need.

During the Ceremony, the Mother of the Bride

1. May assist in last-minute ceremony troubleshooting.

2. Is escorted down the aisle by an usher, son, or your father, to her seat immediately before the ceremony begins for a Christian ceremony. If the ceremony is Jewish, she will walk down the aisle with you and your father to stand beneath the huppah.

3. Will be escorted back down the aisle after the ceremony if you are having a Christian ceremony. If your ceremony is Jewish, she will walk in the recessional with your father.

4. Stands in the receiving line with you and your husband after the ceremony.

After the Ceremony, the Mother of the Bride

1. May assist in coordinating vendors at the reception

2. Sits in an honored place at the parents' table

3. May host a post-wedding brunch or afternoon tea

The Bride's Father

Your father's function in your wedding will largely depend on how much he wants to be involved and how much you want him involved. There are no hard and fast rules for the father of the bride assisting in the planning of the wedding, but there is also nothing to say he should not. Traditionally, the father of the bride has the following responsibilities:

Before the Wedding, the Father of the Bride

1. Hosts an engagement party to celebrate the upcoming nuptials. The bride's family traditionally hosts the first engagement party.

2. Customarily contributes financially to the wedding budget

3. May assist you and your fiancé in choosing the venue for your wedding ceremony and for the reception

4. Rents his own tuxedo and may assist with the rental coordination of the best man and the groomsmen

5. Assists in picking up out-of-town guests as they arrive from the airport and shuttling them to their hotel. He may also help arrange

transportation to and from the wedding and reception.

During the Ceremony, the Father of the Bride

1. May escort your mother to her seat immediately before the ceremony for Christian ceremonies, though it is appropriate for a son or usher to do this instead. For Jewish ceremonies, your father will walk with you and your mother down the aisle to stand beneath the huppah.

2. May "give you away" to your fiancé during the ceremony.

3. Will escort your mother down the aisle after the ceremony if you are having a Christian ceremony. If your ceremony is Jewish, he will walk in the recessional with your mother.

4. Stands in the receiving line with you and your husband after the ceremony.

After the Ceremony, the Father of the Bride

1. May choose to give a welcome speech.

2. Sits in an honored place at the parents' table.

3. Toasts you and your husband after the best man's speech.

4. Will dance the traditional father and daughter dance at the reception.

5. May pay remaining vendor fees at the end of the reception.

6. May host a post-wedding brunch or afternoon tea with your mother.

The Groom's Mother

Take some time to talk with your future mother-in-law and customize a personal approach to her role in your wedding.

Before the Wedding, the Mother of the Groom

1. May choose to contact your mother, if they have not previously met, to set up a luncheon or another first meeting. If they are acquainted, she still may choose to set up a luncheon to celebrate.

2. Should attend an engagement party.

3. May decide to host a secondary engagement party after your family's party is complete.

4. May contribute to the wedding budget.

5. Will assist your fiancé with a guest list from their side of the family.

6. May discuss possibilities of different types of ceremonies with you, including family or traditional customs.

7. May help you shop for and choose your wedding gown if you feel comfortable with her.

8. Chooses her dress for the ceremony. She may coordinate formality and color with the mother of the bride.

9. Will plan and host the rehearsal dinner.

During the Ceremony, the Mother of the Groom

1. Is escorted down the aisle by an usher, son, or your fiancé's father to her seat immediately before the ceremony begins for a Christian ceremony. If the ceremony is Jewish, she will walk down the aisle with your fiancé and his father to stand beneath the huppah.

2. Will be escorted back down the aisle after the ceremony if you are having a Christian ceremony. If your ceremony is Jewish, she will walk in the recessional with your fiancé's father.

3. Stands in the receiving line with you and your husband after the ceremony.

After the Ceremony, the Mother of the Groom

1. Sits in an honored place at the parents' table

2. Dances with your fiancé during the mother and son dance

3. Attends the post-wedding brunch your mother and father hosts and hosts one herself with your fiancé's father

The Groom's Father

You and your fiancé can bring your future father-in-law into the planning of the wedding if you so choose and if he would like to help. The traditional role of the groom's father is as follows.

Before the Wedding, the Father of the Groom

1. Should attend the engagement party

2. May assist your fiancé's mother in hosting a secondary engagement party after your family's hosted party

3. May contribute to the wedding budget

4. Will rent his own tuxedo

5. Will help plan and host the rehearsal dinner

6. May travel with your fiancé and the best man to the ceremony

During the Ceremony the Father of the Groom

1. May escort your fiancé's mother down the aisle to her seat immediately before the ceremony begins, if it is a Christian ceremony. Alternately, an usher or another son may perform this duty. If the ceremony is Jewish, he will walk down the aisle with your fiancé and his mother to stand beneath the huppah.

2. Will escort your fiancé's mother back down the aisle after the ceremony if you are having a Christian ceremony. If your ceremony is Jewish, he will walk in the recessional with your fiancé's mother.

3. Stands in the receiving line with you and your husband after the ceremony.

After the Ceremony the Father of the Groom

1. Sits in an honored place at the parents' table

2. May make a welcoming speech

3. May toast you and your fiancé

4. May pay off remaining balances with wedding vendors

5. Hosts the post-wedding brunch

If you prefer minimal assistance from your parents, be sure to communicate your wishes clearly from the beginning.

∾ *Final Thoughts* ∾

Friends and family are normally more than willing to help and are thrilled to be asked to be in your wedding party. Do not hesitate to ask for help when you find yourself becoming overwhelmed. By communicating your wishes to your wedding party from the beginning, the wedding planning will be that much easier. The difference it will make in your sanity, your budget, and your wedding will surprise you.

Location, Location, Location

You want to find the perfect place to exchange your vows and celebrate your marriage afterward, within your budget. Consider the size and formality of your wedding when deciding on a venue.

Certain locations are simply going to cost more, regardless of the season, day, or time, than other locations. Discuss with your fiancé exactly what is important to each of you before you begin searching. At this point, you should have a budget amount allocated for the ceremony and reception locations. The more time you have to find your location, the better savings you are likely to find. Start early.

Your Wedding Ceremony

The location for your wedding ceremony can be almost anywhere — a church, synagogue, cathedral, or other religious venue. It can be in your home, a park, on the waterfront, in a garden, or in your parents' backyard. What you should consider first is whether you and your fiancé want to have a religious or a civil ceremony.

Religious Ceremonies

Religious ceremonies are the most popular types of weddings, coming in at 75 percent. Naturally, most religious ceremonies take place in a house of worship, such as a church or synagogue.

Your religious selection will depend on you and your fiancé's affiliation with a particular house of worship. You should arrange an appointment with the clergy to discuss the services. Requirements for religious ceremonies differ widely from one church to another, so it is in your best interest to set up a meeting as soon as possible.

You and your fiancé may be required to undergo premarital counseling, take specific premarital classes, and meet with your officiant several times before your wedding ceremony. If the house of worship you and your fiancé have set your heart on is not available on your wedding date, you can either change your wedding date, or you can continue looking at other possible locations.

Do not be surprised at the fees you may be charged at your church or other house of worship for your ceremony. Often there are fees for setting up and taking down any decorations and for cleanup. If the church organist is participating, expect a fee. Be sure to ask for a list of all fees when meeting with the clergy who will perform your ceremony.

Even if you and your fiancé are not a member of a house of worship, you can still have your ceremony in one. Realize, however, there will likely be additional fees for non-members. Also, members will frequently have the first pick of wedding dates, so you may need to plan further ahead.

Civil Ceremonies

A civil wedding ceremony is performed by a judge, justice of the peace, a county official, or other officiant, often in a non-religious setting. About 25 percent of all wedding ceremonies are civil ceremonies, and if this is your and your fiancé's choice, you will have to investigate your area's legal requirements, as they vary from state to state.

With a civil ceremony, you and your fiancé have a variety of possibilities for the location. Most judges will travel to locations other than the courthouse to perform the ceremony; check whether travel is possible.

An advantage to having a civil ceremony is that it allows a more personalized ceremony, one that is exactly right for your marriage.

Officiant Information

If you and your fiancé have decided on a civil ceremony, you may be wondering how you will find an officiant. There are several sources available to you.

♥ **Venue Vendor Lists** — As you narrow down your search for a ceremony site, ask to see their vendor lists. Most, if not all, ceremony locations will offer such a list. The lists will have caterers, florists, and officiants.

♥ **The Internet** — Search for city, state wedding officiants. If your ceremony is going to be in a smaller community, try searching for the closest big city to your venue.

♥ **The National Association of Wedding Officiants** — If you search by state, you will be able to locate names of officiants in your area. Do not worry if you do not see your locale listed; the site has an online form you can fill out, and someone will then send you a list of possibilities.

♥ **The Telephone Book** — Flip through the Yellow Pages under "clergy" and "wedding" to gather some names in your area.

♥ **Nondenominational Churches** — You may find officiants at nondenominational churches who will be happy to conduct a ceremony for you and your fiancé at another venue.

When you begin to narrow down your officiant choices, whether for a religious or a civil ceremony, you will want to ask them the following questions:

❤ What is the expected honorarium, donation, or fee amount? Find out ahead of time whom you pay it to and when.

❤ If your officiant is traveling to your location, does he or she charge any traveling fees?

❤ For religious ceremonies, is premarital counseling involved?

❤ Can you write your own wedding vows, or does the officiant supply the vows? Is it your choice?

❤ Is the officiant licensed to perform in the county where you are being married?

❤ Will he or she provide services for the wedding rehearsal? If so, are there extra fees involved?

Whether your ceremony is going to be civil or religious, it is traditional to pay the officiant an honorarium fee. At times, this is a donation made to the house of worship; other times it is simply a separate fee. Your officiant will cost you anywhere from $100-600 or more. Comparison shop for your officiant to get a price that fits in your wedding budget.

Your Wedding Ceremony Worksheet

Use this worksheet to determine whether you and your fiancé want to have a religious or a civil ceremony. It will also assist you in planning the basic details of your ceremony and the type of venue:

	Your Wedding Ceremony		Location of Ceremony
	Religious Ceremony		Inside a House of Worship
	Civil (Secular) Ceremony		Indoors
	Long and Symbolic		Outdoors
	Short but Sweet		Civil Venue (Courtroom)

YOUR WEDDING CEREMONY		LOCATION OF CEREMONY	
	Somewhere in the Middle		Other:
	Other:		Other:

WEDDING CEREMONY RITUALS		JEWISH RITUALS	
	Traditional Vows		Ketubah
	Originally Written Vows		B'deken (veiling of Bride)
	Ring Exchange		Sheva Brachot
	Readings — Poetry or Verse		Breaking the Glass
	Soloist		Huppah
	Unity Candle		Tish
	Marriage Contract		Kiddushin
	Wine Sharing		Yichud
	Offering to Ancestors		Other:
	Moment of Silence		Other:

REMARRIAGE RITUALS		OTHER: PERSONAL	
	Family Vows		
	Family Unity Candle		
	Family Exchange of Ring		
	Other:		

YOUR WEDDING GUESTS		YOUR WEDDING PARTY	
	Couple and Family Only		Bride's Attendant #:
	Small Guest List		Groom's Attendant #:
	Medium Guest List		Parents:
	All Reception Guests		Stepparents:
	Must Accomodate:		**Budget: $**

When you and your fiancé know what type of wedding ceremony you want, it is time to begin searching for your location. This can be exciting, nerve-wracking, and time consuming. The following information will help you get started:

Sources

When you begin searching for the venue for your ceremony, there are sources for affordable rates and sites.

1. **Visitors and Tourism Bureaus** provide online information. They customarily offer a guide to local facilities that are available for wedding ceremonies and receptions at low, and sometimes, no cost.

2. **The Chamber of Commerce** in your locality will have a guide on not only wedding and reception venues, but also on various wedding vendors, including florists, bakers, caterers, and photographers. You should be able to find more information online.

3. **Parks Departments** are incredible resources if you and your fiancé are interested in an outdoor wedding ceremony. You will want to ask about popular wedding sites in local parks.

4. **Web sites** can give you local information. Do a search under city, state wedding venues.

Continuing Your Search

As you begin to consider specific locations, it is important to be aware of all the different issues you may come up against. The following information will assist you and your fiancé in knowing what to look for and what to ask.

- ♥ Start your search far in advance; you are more apt to find what you want, on the date you want it, for the price you want it.

- ♥ If you are having a religious ceremony in a location other than a house of worship, seek the permission of your officiant.

- ♥ Know how many guests you are inviting when you begin searching. You want to be sure the space you select has enough room for your guest list.

❤ Are all the necessary facilities in place? Restrooms, electricity, ample parking, handicapped access, and any other facility you and your fiancé deem as a necessity?

❤ Does the location have seating available for your use, or will you have to rent chairs for your guests? Renting chairs can be an expensive proposition.

❤ Ascertain if there is ample time allowed for your ceremony. One thing you do not want on your wedding day is to feel rushed.

❤ For an outdoor wedding, visit the site during the season and at the time of day your wedding ceremony will take place.

❤ Listen for traffic noise. Be sure the sounds will not intrude.

Questions to Ask Your Wedding Ceremony Venue

When you visit locations, bring a list of questions. If you do not ask, you may end up spending far more money than you planned, simply because you were not aware.

❤ Is the site available on your wedding date?

❤ Is there a standard fee charged? What is it?

❤ What does the site supply? Find out what you will have to bring on your own so you can plan your rental fees.

❤ Are there any restrictions involved in decorating the site?

❤ Are there any additional fees involved in decorating the site?

❤ When can you decorate? How long before the ceremony?

❤ Are there any additional restrictions or fees in cleanup after the ceremony?

♥ Are there any rules you need to know regarding photography, videography, candles, flowers, or anything else that may add on additional fees?

♥ Does it charge an extra fee if you hire an outside musician, soloist, or organist?

♥ If the site is outdoors, do you need to purchase a special permit to have your ceremony there?

♥ Who is your contact person? Ask for name, e-mail, and phone number. Will you be charged a fee for questions?

♥ Is there any discount or savings plan?

Cost-Saving Locations

Later in this chapter, receptions are covered in more detail; however, you can have a breathtaking, absolutely beautiful location for your ceremony and your reception by considering alternative sites. For example, restaurants, galleries, country clubs, community centers, and museums often offer reasonable rates for wedding ceremonies and receptions. When you begin searching for economical locations, the following places may be perfect for you and your fiancé.

♥ Contact your local historical society and ask if any of your area's mansions are available for a wedding ceremony or reception. You could hold the festivities either indoors or outside if the home has gardens. Frequently, they are available for a reasonable fee given as a donation to the historical society.

♥ When you speak with the historical society, ask for recommendations on free wedding locations. Its staff members know your locality well and may be able to direct you to the perfect place.

♥ You or your fiancé's alma mater's banquet hall is another great place to consider. As an alumnus of the school, you may find you have access to university locales at a terrific price. Ask your alumni president's office for a contact.

♥ Were you or your fiancé in the military? If so, a military chapel is another consideration. As a veteran, you may find a great deal.

♥ If your family or friends have a vacation home on the lake, the ocean, in the mountains, or another beautiful spot, find out if you can use it for your ceremony and your reception. One word of caution: ascertain that any rental equipment you need to pay for does not end up costing more than a venue with everything you need included in its price.

♥ Waterfront wedding ceremonies are still one of the most romantic locations. Although you will have to pay for a license, it will be nominal.

♥ Do you live near an arboretum? For autumn, spring, and summer weddings, you will not be disappointed in the view. Plus, the price may be exactly right.

Cost-Savings Tips While You Search

There are always ways to save money. Some require little more than common sense, and others require a bit of creative thinking.

♥ Comparison shop.

♥ Consider having your ceremony and reception in the same venue. You will save money by having only one rental fee, and you will save time in transportation.

♥ Do not pay the religious adviser's fee, which can begin at $75. Instead, if you and your fiancé require a little research on the religious elements of your ceremony, speak directly with the officiant.

♥ Try not to spend extra money on ceremonial items, such as a ring bearer's pillow, aisle runner, or a unity candle. Instead, many churches will lend them. Another possibility is to have skilled friends and family make what you need. You can save hundreds of dollars by not purchasing these items.

♥ If you or your fiancé needs to provide proof of annulment or divorce, do not hire the church to locate your legal paperwork. Send for the copies yourself.

♥ If you and your fiancé are required to attend premarital classes, comparison shop to find the best price. Before signing, ascertain if your church will accept a certificate of completion from another church.

♥ Always ask about any extra fees. You may be surprised at the total tally if you do not go over it with your officiant and your venue.

♥ Do not accept a standby position on a location schedule. With all the planning you are putting into your wedding, the last thing you need on your wedding day is no location.

♥ If you pay a deposit to hold a location and then decide on another, be sure that you will get your deposit back. Do not give a nonrefundable deposit unless you are 100 percent sure of it.

♥ Ask about discounts. Sometimes, you will not know there are any discounts available unless you ask.

♥ Consider having a friend or family member officiate. This will add a special extra to your ceremony and, in most states, it is easy to become licensed for one day to perform weddings.

♥ Fees paid to a house of worship may be considered a charitable contribution, which means a tax deduction. Ask your accountant or tax preparer if this will apply to you.

With proper planning, organization, and research, you and your fiancé will find the perfect location for your ceremony and stick to your budget.

⊰ Your Reception Location ⊱

Your reception is the place of celebration for your marriage. It is an important venue, and there is plenty to think about when selecting the right one. Many of the suggestions already mentioned in this chapter for ceremony locations are also terrific reception locales, so be sure to review that section thoroughly as well as this one.

Your reception venue should be a reflection of you and your fiancé's personal style. It will also dictate much of the planning that will happen in the months before your wedding. For this reason, you should begin your search early for the right venue for your reception. Just as with your wedding ceremony location, you will save more money if you have ample time before your ceremony to select your reception site.

Your Reception Location Worksheet

You and your fiancé need to decide on some details before you begin searching for your reception locale. The following reception location worksheet should help you both figure it out:

LOCATION USES		LOCATION SERVICES	
	Ceremony and Reception		Food Included with Site
	Reception Only		No Food, Bring Own/Caterer
	Changing Clothes		Chairs/Tables Included
	Dancing		Rentals Required
	Other:		Other:

LOCATION DETAILS		LOCATION FEATURES	
	Can Walk from Ceremony		Beautiful Interiors
	Proximity to Ceremony		Near the Water
	Indoors		Under Tent
	Outdoors		Daylight Features
	Indoor and Outdoor		Evening Features
	Other:		The View

Location Style		Location Special Requirements	
	Antique/Old-World		Handicapped Access
	Modern		A Coat Check
	Formal		Children's Area
	Casual and Intimate		Parking
	Fun and Jazzy		Other:
	Other:		Other:
	Must Accommodate:		**Budget:**

Cost-Saving Tips While You Search

Choosing your reception location does not have to mean a ridiculous amount of money out of your wedding budget. There are savings to be found, if you know where to look, what questions to ask, and how to find the best deals.

Most of what you need to know about finding your reception site is in the prior section on ceremony sites, as much of the information is exactly the same. Below, you will find specific information to include with what has already been covered.

❤ Ignore high-profile ads for reception halls. These places are unlikely to offer any savings, as they are considered prime reception locations.

❤ To avoid high-priced rental fees, focus your attention on reception halls that already have tables, chairs, linens, and other equipment included in their cost.

❤ Comparison shop in every step of your planning. Keep notes on what you see, what your impressions are, and any other bit of information you learn about the establishment.

❤ Unless your heart is completely set on crystal, ultra-fine linens, and other pricey extras, take some time to look at smaller banquet halls. Often, their prices are much more reasonable. You may have to trim your guest list, but that will give you increased savings elsewhere.

❤ If you do choose a home reception or another location that will require you to rent equipment, keep accurate lists so when you begin comparing prices, you know exactly what you need.

❤ Although an outdoor location is a beautiful option, do not forget that if the weather does not cooperate, you will need an alternate location. Some venues offer both outdoor and indoor locales for the same price; check into this, as it will save you money, time, and stress.

Questions to Ask Your Wedding Reception Venue

When you visit various reception venues, be sure to bring a list of questions with you. Being informed is one of the best methods of staying on top of any hidden costs, stresses, or other issues that a locale could cause.

❤ Is it available on your wedding date?

❤ Is there a set amount of hours you will have access to the venue? If you run over, are there additional fees?

❤ What is the structure of its costs? Flat fee, per head, by the hour, or a combination?

❤ Do you have to use its in-house caterer, or can you hire your own? Are there fees associated with either scenario?

❤ Does the venue have a liquor license? Must you purchase from its bar, or can you supply the alcohol for your reception?

❤ Ask where the buffet is set up and other logistic questions. If possible, try to visit the location when it is set up for a wedding reception.

❤ What is the staff-to-guest ratio?

❤ What is provided? Remember, the more provided in the basic cost, the better for your budget.

♥ Are there enough outlets for lighting, equipment, and audio requirements?

♥ Is there a dance floor, or does one need to be brought in? If there is not a dance floor, can the venue arrange to have one brought in? Is there an additional fee?

♥ Are there restrictions on decorations, dress code, or music?

♥ Are there enough restrooms for your number of guests? Are they clean? Will staff be on hand to keep them clean during the celebration?

♥ Is there enough parking, and is the entrance easy to access from the parking lot?

♥ Are any other wedding ceremonies and/or receptions going on at the same time as yours? On the same day? Is there any chance that you will have difficulty having the appropriate access to decorate and set up?

♥ Ask for references of past gatherings. If you can get them, this will be a valuable resource for you.

♥ Will the manager be on hand throughout the entire event? Does he or she seem flexible and likeable?

♥ Does the venue have liability insurance?

The Home Wedding Ceremony and Reception

If all the above fills you with fear, you may consider holding your wedding ceremony and reception at your home. Although this may seem like the easiest and the least expensive option, it may not be. Take the following into consideration before deciding a home wedding ceremony and/or reception is right for you.

Your Time

You are already planning your own wedding and reception. This means your time is going to be limited. Hosting the ceremony and your reception at your home adds another entire set of planning onto your already full schedule. Of course, you can make it work, as long as you realize there are additional steps you will be required to plan. Again, organization will go a long way.

Your Wedding Budget

Depending on your situation, your home, and the assistance of those you know, your inexpensive home ceremony and/or reception could cost quite a bit more than you are expecting. You will likely be required to rent or borrow most of the equipment and amenities you will need: items such as tables, chairs, tents, dishware, flatware, glassware, and a dance floor, for example. Points to consider when determining if your home or another home is a location that will work for your ceremony and/or reception:

❤ Evaluate the size of the house.

> ❤ Take a walk through the home and try to visualize it as a venue for your ceremony and/or reception.

> ❤ Decide if you want an indoor or outdoor ceremony and/or reception.

> ❤ Carry a pad of paper and a pen with you to jot ideas down as you think of them.

❤ Evaluate the kitchen.

> ❤ Is it large enough to prepare the food for your reception?

> ❤ If you are hiring a caterer, will it accommodate a catering staff?

> ❤ Does the kitchen have the proper equipment necessary? Are

there enough ovens, sinks, counter space, and refrigerators/
freezers? One average-sized refrigerator may not be large
enough to hold all the wedding day food.

♥ Evaluate the yard.

   ♥ Is there a suitable location large enough for the ceremony or
   the reception tables?

   ♥ Is there a level area to put up a rented tent?

   ♥ Is there a level area for your dance floor?

   ♥ Determine what your backup plan is in case of inclement
   weather. Where will you go if it is too hot, too cold, or
   raining?

♥ Evaluate the indoor space.

   ♥ Is there a large enough space to hold the number of guests
   you have invited?

   ♥ Will furniture need to be rearranged to make room for
   additional seating for the ceremony and for the reception?

   ♥ Will you need to find a storage facility to store the furniture, or
   is there room in a basement or another room in the home?

♥ Is there proper temperature control: air conditioning for hot summer
days and heat control for cool weather?

♥ Is the floor plan sufficient for mingling guests and wait staff?
Remember, the hallways need to be large enough for people to pass
by each other easily, often holding food and beverages.

♥ Where will the disc jockey or band set up? Do you have all the
necessary amenities? Consider power outlets, a stage, and a sound
system.

♥ Do you have space to set up a bar?

♥ Does the home have easily accessible bathrooms for the number of guests who will be in attendance?

♥ If you have overnight guests attending, is there room for them, or will they need to stay in a hotel?

♥ Are there enough changing rooms for the entire wedding party?

♥ Parking space can often be an issue. Is there sufficient space for your guests to park their cars nearby?

♥ Talk to your neighbors, especially if they are not invited. Be sure they will not complain about crowded parking, delivery trucks, or music being played in the evening.

If, after reading the above, you and your fiancé have decided a home wedding ceremony and/or reception is exactly right for you, the next step is to consider what rentals you may need. The following checklist will help you narrow it down:

♥ Tents for outdoor ceremonies and/or receptions

♥ Bridal arch for the ceremony

♥ Chairs for your guests for the ceremony

♥ Tables and chairs for your guests for the reception

♥ Tables for a buffet at the reception

♥ China or other dishware

♥ Crystal and glassware

♥ Silverware

♥ Tablecloths, napkins, and other types of linens

♥ Serving platters and bowls

- ♥ Punch bowls and cups

- ♥ An aisle runner for the ceremony

- ♥ A portable bar

- ♥ Installation of a dance floor

- ♥ A platform/stage for the band/disc jockey

⌘ Final Thoughts ⌘

Your wedding ceremony and reception venues are essential to the style, tradition, and celebration you want for your wedding day. Although venues can cost thousands of dollars, you can save money by being flexible, planning ahead, and knowing what questions to ask.

Whether you and your fiancé have decided on a formal wedding ceremony and an elegant reception, an informal and casual gathering, or a relaxed good time, you can achieve it and stick to your budget.

The most important consideration in adhering to your wedding budget will be in giving you and your fiancé ample time to make a decision. The less time you have, the fewer savings.

As soon as you and your fiancé decide on the type of ceremony and location you desire, begin searching for locations. Once you book them, save all documentation, including the contract, fees list, receipts for any payment, and anything that was agreed on. Get it all in writing. Never count on word-of-mouth agreements, or you may get a huge bill.

Attire for the Bride

By now you and your fiancé have chosen the date, time, location, and style of your wedding ceremony and reception. This means it is time to think about attire. As the bride, the number one vision in your mind is your wedding gown. Chances are you have already given considerable thought to your gown, your veil, and even your shoes. For the bride they are often the most thrilling part of planning the wedding.

As much fun as you will have with this, you also have to think about your bridal party, your mother, your fiancé's mother, and the groomsmen. Dressing yourself and your wedding party can be fun, stressful, and exciting, but it is time consuming.

Your Wedding Gown

Your wedding gown is the focal point of your wedding party's attire, as all other attire decisions will stem from the dress you choose. Average prices for a gown range from $650 to $1,500, but you can spend much more than that, up to $15,000. Of course, there are bargains to be found if you know where to look and what to look for.

Choosing Your Gown

The first step is determining what your style is and what the basic fundamentals of your dress will be. Determining the perfect gown for you is actually a series of smaller decisions that will lead you to the gown of your dreams.

The best place to begin is the magazine rack. Head to your nearest bookstore and buy several of the newest wedding magazines. When you flip through the pages, clip out and file anything that you like. If you love the beading on a dress but dislike the neckline — still cut it out. At this stage, you are determining what you like and what you think will look amazing on you, and this may mean different aspects of different gowns.

After you have an assortment of photographs, lay them out in front of you. Write down what appeals to you — length, neckline, color, fabric, beading, gown style. You can also go to bridal shows, watch wedding programs on television, and search the Internet.

Your list will help employees at any of the wedding salons or shops you visit. After trying on several gowns, if you find that what you thought you wanted no longer appeals to you, talk to the consultant. She will be able to give you advice based on your body type, skin tone, and preferences.

Online Sources — Designer Wedding Dresses

In addition to the magazines, the following Web sites are designer wedding gown sites to give you ideas on wedding dresses.

- ♥ Alfred Angelo — **www.alfredangelo.com**

- ♥ Alfred Sung Bridal Collection — **www.alfredsungbridals.com**

- ♥ Alvina Valenta — **www.alvinavalenta.com**

- ♥ Eden Bridals — **www.edenbridals.com**

- ♥ Impression Bridal — **www.impressionbridal.com**

- ♥ Lazaro — **www.lazarobridal.com**

- ♥ Melissa Sweet — **www.melissasweet.com**

- ♥ Paloma Blanca — **http://palomablanca.com**

- ♥ Venus Brides — **www.venusbridal.com**

- ♥ Vera Wang — **www.verawang.com**

Wedding Gown Styles

Before you hit the salons, understanding the various terms associated with wedding gowns will assist you in making a selection.

CASE STUDY: FAIRYTALE WEDDINGS AND BRIDAL

What is your area of expertise?

Specializing in custom-made, inspired replicas of designer styles or clients' own designs. We work with several factories that have many years of experience in producing bridal gowns and evening wear and are actively in the trade, located in China, Japan, Vietnam, North and South Korea, Malaysia, India, and the Phillipines.

CASE STUDY: FAIRYTALE WEDDINGS AND BRIDAL

We offer label gowns, dresses, invitations, wedding-related products, and items at highly discounted prices.

We are a wedding planning, decorating, and rental service company specializing in small to large-sized events.

What are the most common mistakes that result in the bride and groom going over budget?

Favors, videographer, photographer, type of limo they rent.

If you could offer one piece of advice to a couple planning their own wedding under a budget, what would it be?

Be realistic and accept what they can truly afford. The wedding is not about the dress, veil, flowers, favors — it's about their love and commitment to one another and sharing that special moment with relatives and friends.

What are overlooked areas of savings?

Businesses offering options other than the norm for wedding-related items and services.

How do a bride and groom stay on budget?

1) Be realistic and accept what you can truly afford.

2) Plan way ahead.

3) Be organized.

4) Shop around for prices on all products and services.

5) Read all contracts for any facility and vendor before signing.

What is the biggest misconception you see in wedding planning?

The couples think they have to have it all and the best of everything.

How can a couple find quality services at the best price?

Research, making appointments with various vendors in each category that discount, and getting to know them on a personal level. Especially on home-based discount wedding businesses. They hardly have any overhead expenses, which is and can be passed on to the consumer. They are smaller and have the time to give personal attention and quality service. They'd be surprised in what they might find in them.

CASE STUDY: FAIRYTALE WEDDINGS AND BRIDAL

What shouldn't the bride and groom do to cut costs?

Cutting back on the reception facility and quality of menu.

Do you have an example to share that shows how a bride and groom saved money?

Visit our Web site: **http://fairytaleweddingsandbridal.com/ Read%Testimonials.html**.

It's easy to become overwhelmed when planning a wedding. What is your advice for lowering the stress?

Give yourself plenty of time to plan your wedding and to be organized. If the couple's budget permits, hire a wedding coordinator/planner; they are open minded, have many ideas, suggestions, and advice and eliminate the stress from couples and families.

How would a couple know when a price is truly "too good to be true?"

Common sense.

Any other suggestions or advice you would like to share?

Look for alternatives and other options in all areas.

Melody Stiltner

Fairytale Weddings and Bridal

407 Vine Street

Clyde, Ohio 43410

419-547-9827

www.fairytaleweddingsandbridal.com

Silhouette Types

- ♥ **A-Line or Princess dresses** feature vertical seams that flow from the shoulders down to a triangular flared skirt (an "A" shape). This design style is flattering for most body shapes, which makes it one of the most popular for brides.

❤ **Ball Gowns** have a full skirt that begins at the waist and continues to formal length. This style is the most traditional and formal of all wedding dresses. Normally, they have a low or off-the-shoulder neckline, a fitted bodice, and a waistline that leads to a bell-shaped skirt.

❤ **Empire** is characterized by a high waistline right under the bust, which is reminiscent of the early 19th century. Empire gowns can have either a slim or a full skirt.

❤ **Sheath** is a dress with clean lines and classic styling that closely follows the line of the bride's body. It often has a detachable train.

Hem Lengths

❤ **Ankle Length** dresses have a skirt that falls just above the ankles.

❤ **Tea Length** gowns offer a hem that falls several inches above the ankles.

❤ **Floor Length** gowns have a skirt on which the hemline skims the floor.

Sleeves

❤ **Bishop** is a closed, full sleeve that gathers into a narrow cuff.

❤ **Bow** is a short sleeve worn on or off the shoulder, made of a looped fabric.

❤ **Cap** is a small, short sleeve that sits on the shoulder, either forming a cap or falling onto the top of the arm to give minimal coverage.

❤ **Dolman** is a long sleeve that is wide at the top and narrow at the wrist.

❤ **Fitted** is a long, traditional sleeve fitted close to the arm, tapering to the wrist.

❤ **Gigot or Leg-of-Mutton** is a sleeve that is extremely wide over the upper arm and narrow from the elbow to the wrist.

❤ **Juliette** is a long, tight sleeve, with a puff at the top.

❤ **Puffed sleeve** is a short sleeve, gathered at the top and bottom.

Trains

❤ **Sweeping Train** is a short train. It is also known as a brush train, because it barely brushes the floor. The back hem is a few inches lower than the front hem. This type of train is perfect for an elegantly informal or a semiformal wedding gown because it adds the elegance of a train without a large amount of additional fabric.

❤ **Court Train** is a perfect choice for an informal or semiformal ceremony. The train extends about one foot from the hemline or three feet from the waistline.

❤ **Chapel Length Train** is the most common train for wedding gowns because it has all the elegance of a full train but is not overly cumbersome. This type of train extends one and a third to one and a half yards from the hemline and is perfect for semiformal wedding gowns, but it is elegant enough to be used for a formal wedding gown.

❤ **Semi-Cathedral Length Train** is between the length of a chapel and a cathedral train. It extends approximately one and three-quarters to two yards from the hemline. This type of train will work well for a semiformal or a formal wedding gown.

♥ **Cathedral Length Train** is the train of choice for formal weddings and the "princess in a fairy tale" appearance. It often extends two and one half to three yards from the hemline. Gowns with cathedral trains are often available with a bustling option or even a removable train for easier celebrating at the reception.

♥ **Royal Train or Monarch Train** is exactly that. Think of royal wedding gowns, such as Princess Diana's. If you want a gown on which the train extends down the aisle while you are standing at the altar, this is it. This train extends approximately three yards from the waistline.

Wedding Gown Necklines

There are many types of necklines to consider when deciding on a wedding gown. It is helpful to know the terms.

♥ **Bateau Necklines**, sometimes called boat necklines, softly follow the curve of the bride's collarbone. This neckline is high in the front and the back and opens wide at the sides, ending at the shoulder seams.

♥ **Contessa Necklines** are cut about three inches below the shoulder to form a continuous line across the arms and chest. It is normally featured on off-the-shoulder gowns.

♥ **Halter Necklines** feature a sleeveless, shoulder-less dress with a high choked neck.

♥ **Illusion High Necklines** fit snugly on the neck, creating a choker type effect.

♥ **Off-the-Shoulder Necklines** hover gently across the top of the bust line. The shoulders are either uncovered or are covered by a sheer material that is see-through.

♥ **Open Sweetheart Back Yoke**, sometimes called a keyhole back, features a heart-shaped opening that is often fringed with pearls or other beading.

♥ **Portrait Necklines** use a shawl collar that wraps around the shoulders.

♥ **Queen Anne Necklines** cup the sides of the bride's neck and then sculpt down across the chest. They have a high-rising collar at the back of the neckline.

♥ **Sabrina Necklines** have high scoop necks.

♥ **Scoop Necklines** gently slope downward across the bodice in a softly curving line.

♥ **Square Necklines** show an open yoke shaped in the form of a half square.

♥ **Sweetheart Necklines** are one of the most popular of all necklines. They feature an open yoke shaped in the form of the top half of a heart.

♥ **Tank Top Bodices** are sleeveless gowns with a scoop neck.

♥ **U-Scalloped Necklines** feature an open yoke in the shape of a "U" and are embellished with scalloped lace appliqué.

♥ **V-Shaped Necklines** are just as they sound. They feature an open yoke coming to a "V" shape midway down the bodice.

♥ **Wedding Bank Necklines** consist of a gown in which the yoke is either open or is of sheer netting with an ornate band fitted snugly on the neck, creating a choker effect.

Wedding Gown Fabrics

The fabric for your wedding gown is important, not only for your wedding budget, but also on the fit, the comfort, and the overall effect of your gown, as well as the formality or informality of your ceremony. Style, cut, texture, drape, and even the season are essential factors to consider when selecting the best fabric for your gown.

Some fabrics are meant to cling to your body, while others drape or even flare out. The weight of your dress is also affected by the type of fabric it is made from. Below you will find a list of fabrics often used in wedding gown creation.

❤ **Batiste** is a lightweight, transparent, soft fabric, often layered.

❤ **Brocade** is a woven fabric, thick and formal, with raised designs. Popular for fall and winter.

❤ **Charmeuse** is a semi-lustrous soft fabric, is lightweight, and feels like satin.

❤ **Chiffon** is a delicate, sheer, transparent fabric with a soft finish. Chiffon is often layered in overskirts, sheer sleeves, and wraps.

❤ **Crepe** is a thin, soft, light fabric with a crinkled surface.

❤ **Damask** is similar to brocade with raised designs, but it is a much lighter weight.

❤ **Duchesse Satin** is a hybrid of silk and rayon, woven into a lightweight satin finish and is becoming quite popular.

❤ **Dupioni fabric** has a nubby finish, with thick, coarse fibers and a slight sheen.

♥ **Faille** is a slightly shiny fabric, ribbed and available in a variety of fibers.

♥ **Gabardine** is a tightly woven fabric with a firm, durable finish and single diagonal lines on the surface.

♥ **Georgette** is a sheer, lightweight fabric, often made of polyester or silk. The surface is crinkled, much like crepe.

♥ **Grosgrain** is a strong, closely woven corded fabric.

♥ **Illusion** is a sheer net, fine fabric, often used on the sleeves and/or necklines of gowns.

♥ **Jersey** is a elastic knit fabric, with lengthwise ribs on the surface and crosswise ribs on the underside.

♥ **Moire** is a heavy silk taffeta with a wavy, subtle design.

♥ **Organdy** is a transparent, stiff fabric.

♥ **Peau De Soie** is a heavy fabric that is less shiny than satin, of high quality, fine ribs, and a grainy appearance.

♥ **Shantung** is similar to raw silk, has a slightly nubby finish, and is available in silk and polyester.

♥ **Silk Gazar** is a four-ply silk organza.

♥ **Silk Mikado** is a type of blended silk, often heavier than 100 percent silk.

♥ **Silk-faced Satin** has a glossy front and a matte back; this fabric is a smooth silk-satin.

♥ **Taffeta** is a crisp, smooth fabric with a slight rib and a moderate sheen.

♥ **Tulle** is a netting made of silk, nylon, or rayon and is used primarily for skirts and bridal veils.

♥ **Velvet** is a fabric with a soft, thick nap and is used mostly for winter weddings.

Body Type and Gown Style

At this stage, you will find it helpful to know what style of gown will be the most flattering to your figure. Some body types just do not do well in certain styles of dresses; this is an area you should consider before hitting the wedding salons. On your wedding day, you want to look as stunning as possible, and you should.

All women are shaped differently, so no styles are meant for everyone. Use the following chart to help you narrow down the best style of wedding gown for your body type.

IF YOU ARE	WHAT IS THE BEST GOWN FOR YOU:
Slender/Short	Simple styles are best. A straight or slight A-Line dress will add height. A gown with Princess seams that is not too full will also make you look taller.
Avoid	Dresses with heavy beadwork or beaded lace, as this will camouflage the Princess seams, having the opposite effect. Also, stay away from overly full or puffed sleeves, which will make you appear wider and shorter. Gathered or tiered skirts will also appear to minimize your height.
Full-figured/Short	Seek out styles that will make your figure appear longer and leaner. Vertical silhouette lines, such as the A-Line, Princess, and straight styles will help achieve this. Look for gowns that skim your body and flow without hugging your curves too much.

IF YOU ARE	WHAT IS THE BEST GOWN FOR YOU:
Avoid	Heavy, shiny fabrics tend to make the body look heavier. Bouffant or tiered silhouettes and an overly full veil should be avoided, as they will give the illusion of added bulk. Stay away from larger prints, even in the same color.
Average/Average	Congratulations, your body shape is the one most designers target. You have many more options available to you, but consider gowns with defined waistlines and gathered skirts. The sheath and fitted gowns are good choices.
Avoid	Nothing to steer clear from. Try on a few styles and see which flatter your exact body shape the best.
Full-figured/Average	Styles that will be the most slenderizing are the A-Line, Princess, and Empire gowns. Keep an eye out for dresses that flow easily over the hips and do not gather tightly around the waist. Any of the lighter, thin, and soft fabrics will be the most attractive.
Avoid	Stay away from large and small prints. Also, heavier fabrics, as well as heavily beaded gowns, should be avoided. Round necklines may not be the most appealing, depending on the shape of your face.
Slender/Tall	Almost any of the standard styles will be appealing on this body type. If you are slender, you may want to consider dresses that extend past the silhouette. Tiered skirts, French bustles, and beaded laces will add fullness to a slender figure.
Avoid	For brides who do not want to appear taller than they already are, sheath-style gowns should be avoided, as well as any other straight-falling dress. Another consideration — shorter veils, such as the blush veil, may appear too short as compared to the height of a tall bride.
Full-figured/Tall	The full-figured tall bride will want to look for slenderizing styles of gowns. The A-Line, Princess, and Empire gowns are all excellent choices, as they will accentuate the height of the bride and help her appear slimmer.

IF YOU ARE	WHAT IS THE BEST GOWN FOR YOU:
Avoid	Heavier fabrics, heavy beading, full skirts, puffed sleeves, and gathered waists will likely not be the best choices. Anything that adds bulk or clutter will make the full-figured bride appear larger than she actually is.
Plus-Sized	For the plus-size bride, the most appealing wedding gown styles are the simplest styles. Princess seams, A-Line gowns, and Empire-styled gowns will be slenderizing and are fabulous choices.
Avoid	Clingy fabrics, tight-fitting gowns, anything that overly accentuate curves. Also, gathered skirts, textured and printed fabrics, and overly long trains should be avoided.

There are wedding gowns available for all body shapes. The right dress will make you feel like the belle of the ball — which is exactly how it should be on your wedding day.

The Bridal Salon

Whether or not you ultimately purchase your dress from a bridal salon, it is a good place to start. You will be able to try on many different gowns and get a firm idea of what you want. Do not plan on purchasing your dress when you first get started; instead, think of this as wedding gown reconnaissance. Your goal is to narrow down your choices, decide on the exact types of gowns you want, and then take that information away so you can find the best price possible.

You will want to start this process, if possible, at least six months before your wedding date. The sooner you start, the better, for savings and for your sanity. Even if your wedding is a year away, beginning this process now will save you money.

Choose two or three bridal shops and call to make an appointment. Give yourself a slot of at least two hours, and make the appointments during the week when the shops are not busy. Ideally, you will want these first shops to have a wide variety of designers and gowns on hand to give you the broadest spectrum.

Questions to Ask Bridal Salons about Your Wedding Gown

As you call and visit the bridal salons you are most interested in, bring along these questions to ask:

- ♥ What size sample dresses are available? Most stores carry sample dresses in sizes 8 through 10 only, so it is good to know before you go.

- ♥ Will you be able to browse through their selection of dresses yourself, or will the salesperson bring them out to you? It is always better to be able to browse yourself.

- ♥ If you are interested in specific designers, be sure the salons you are considering shopping in have them on hand. List your favorite designers before calling or visiting.

- ♥ What is your budgeted price range for a wedding gown? Do these shops carry dresses within this price range?

- ♥ Some salons have shoes and undergarments available for you to try on along with the gowns you select. Inquire ahead, so you know if you need to bring along your own accessories.

- ♥ If there is a specific dress you are interested in trying on but the salon does not carry it, is it able to order a sample dress for you to try on? Be sure you stipulate "to try on" rather than purchase. Also ascertain that you will not be required to purchase any dresses ordered for you to try on.

♥ Find out how long it will be for a dress to come in after you order it. Normally, it can be anywhere from three to four months, but it always pays to ask. If you need it sooner, can the salon place a rush on it?

♥ Even if the salon does have a sample dress for you to try on, find out if you can get a swatch of the fabric from the dress. Often, sample gowns have lost some of their luster because of continuous use.

♥ If you are interested in purchasing all your wedding attire needs in one location (not recommended), find out if the salon you are interested in carries everything you would need.

♥ Find out if you will receive a written alteration estimate before the dress arrives. If their procedure is to wait until the gown arrives, ask for a basic alteration price list so you are not taken unaware.

♥ Ask about group discounts. If your bridal party girls order their dresses through the same salon, will you receive significant savings?

♥ Find out if the sales consultant will offer recommendations based on your wish list of styles, fabrics, and formality.

When You Visit a Bridal Salon

Bring your wedding dress clippings, along with a list of gown styles, fabrics, and trains you like. Share your vision of your wedding with the sales consultant. She should know the time of year your ceremony will take place , the time of day, if your wedding is formal, semiformal, or informal, inside or out. Give her all the details. She should also know what your budget is. You are not purchasing a gown at this point, but it is still helpful to try on only those in your budget.

Bring the following with you

1. Strapless bra if you are considering a sleeveless dress

2. Shoes with the same heel height you will wear at the ceremony

3. Any other undergarments you will likely wear: pantyhose, tights, and even girdles

4. Another person, someone to tell you what looks good and what does not, and to be a sounding board

When you feel comfortable that the consultant assisting you knows your likes and dislikes, has looked at the pictures you have clipped out, and has read your list of styles and fabrics, the fun begins.

Wedding Salon Tips

Shopping around for your wedding gown is a time-consuming process. The following helpful hints will get you started.

1. The process of finding a gown is exhausting; take frequent breaks. Instead of hitting several shops in one day, spread them out over a couple of weeks. You will find this helpful because you will have more energy, and you will have more time to think about the gown styles you liked the most.

2. Many brides purchase the first dress they try on. Although there is something magical about this, realize that the salons you are visiting know this. Staff are more likely to hand you a expensive gown to try on first for this reason.

3. Stick to your budget and be sure the sales consultant knows you mean it. If you do not want to spend more than $700 for a gown, do not try on any gowns that cost more than this unless you are considering having a gown made or are considering ordering the same dress from a discount retailer and you need to know how it looks on you.

4. If you have your heart set on a strapless gown, be sure to choose one with detachable straps. This way, when you are dancing the night away with your new husband, you will not have to worry about a mishap.

5. Understand that the wedding gown industry follows a completely different size chart, so what your normal size is will not be the case for your wedding gown. Many shops suggest you order a dress several sizes larger than your actual size, but what tends to happen is an expensive alteration bill at the end of your fitting. Ask to see the manufacturer's sizing chart for any dress you are considering purchasing. Then, insist on being measured with a vinyl tape measure, including your bust, waist, hips, and the hollow to hem measurement (from the base of your throat to the hemline). Given your measurements, choose whichever size most closely matches your largest measurement.

If you are measuring yourself or having a friend help you, follow these guidelines:

♥ **Bust/Chest** — Lift your arms straight out from your body (like a "T"), and measure around your body, over the fullest portion of your chest. Do not pull the measuring tape too tight, and wear only your bra.

♥ **Waist** — Keeping a finger between your body and the measuring tape, measure around your waistline.

❤ **Hip** — Press your heels together and measure around your body, crossing over the fullest part of your hip.

❤ **Hollow to Hem** — Stand straight and measure from the base of your throat to where you want your hemline to reach. If in doubt when ordering your dress, go a bit longer so it can be altered.

6. If the salon you visit has a sample gown to try on and it seems too loose, it may not be. Sample gowns tend to get stretched with constant wear and from many different body shapes trying them on. This is why it is best to be measured for your gown.

7. Some salons keep the merchandise in a back room and do not allow you to browse through their selection. Instead, your consultant will ask you for your likes and dislikes and bring you gowns to try on. Try to steer clear of salons that have this practice, as it is always better to see for yourself.

Ways to Save on Your Wedding Gown

The number one way you will save money on your wedding gown is by starting early. There is no such thing as "too early" when trying to get the best deals. When you are pinched for time with the ceremony right around the corner, you are likely to spend a great deal more money than you originally budgeted.

When you begin shopping around, try to avoid the big, fancy wedding salons. Sure, they may have everything you need, but that comes with a price tag. The larger salons often carry the same dresses for more money than you would pay elsewhere. After all, they need money to pay for their plush surroundings. If you can resist purchasing a dress from one of the larger salons and you just want to go for the experience, you can certainly do that. Use them as your first stop in your reconnaissance shopping.

When you are ready to begin seriously shopping, consider these alternate locations and methods for finding the dress of your dreams:

♥ Boutique-style wedding salons offer beautiful dresses at a fraction of the cost. Because their store space is smaller and less elegant, they do not have as much of an overhead, which means their dresses will likely cost less money.

♥ Check out bridal shops in a different part of town, city, or state. Affluent areas will have bloated prices on everything, including wedding gowns. Search for shops in middle-class areas, and you could see significant savings. Although it may not be easy to travel to another state, if you have friends or family spread around the country, you can have them do some shopping for you.

♥ Major department stores normally have bridal departments that are likely to be less expensive, and they have amazing sales throughout the year. Call and find out when they normally mark down their bridal selection.

♥ Attend designer trunk shows and sample sales, an amazing way to get your hands on a designer gown at a fraction of the cost. Look in bridal magazines, bridal Web sites, and in your newspaper's bridal inserts for dates and locations.

♥ Stroll through the fine-dress department at major department stores. A wedding gown may not be labeled a wedding gown. There are many dresses available that may be perfect for your semiformal or informal wedding, so do not discount this idea. You may also find bridesmaids' dresses in this fashion.

♥ You can save money by purchasing your dress at an outlet store. The Yellow Pages and the Internet are great places to begin.

♥ If you are a traditional bride, consider shopping at an antique store. You can find breathtaking dresses for budget prices if you are willing to look. If you locate the perfect dress but it needs refurbishing, check out the cleaning and alteration costs before buying.

♥ Newspaper classified ads are another place to find great deals. For whatever reason, many women decide to part with their wedding dress. You will be surprised at the bargains you can find.

♥ Consignment shops often have brand-new dresses that have never been worn that you can get at a fantastic price. Sometimes a bride purchases her gown and then the wedding is canceled. Instead of having it hang in her closet, she tries to sell it. You can even leave your name and phone number at area consignment shops, and they will be happy to phone you if a dress comes in.

♥ Consider renting your wedding gown. If you are not too fussy about keeping your gown forever, this may be a terrific option for you. There are rental companies all over the country, and they often have some of the newest designs in stock. Instead of spending thousands on the dress of your dreams, you could rent it for about $200.

♥ Have your dress custom made. Although this will not save you as much as some of the other ideas, you can hire a seamstress or a dressmaker to make your gown from scratch and save a decent amount off the store-bought prices. This is especially true if you provide the materials for the gown. Plus, your dress will be custom made to your body shape.

♥ The Internet. Do a search for bargain wedding gowns, and you will get a variety of online shops to browse.

♥ Borrowing a dress. If you do not mind the idea, ask married friends and family members who are about the same size/body shape as you are and find out if they would mind lending you their gown. If you are on an exceptionally tight budget, this may be the best idea.

❤ Check with nearby seamstresses to see if they have a selection of wedding gowns they made or purchased wholesale. This is a more common occurrence than you may think, and often, you can grab them up at an incredible price.

❤ Auctions and flea markets. There are home auctions where everything inside the home is auctioned off in an outdoor area. You may be able to find antique wedding gowns there. In addition, antique flea markets are popping up everywhere, and you could land a vintage wedding gown at a great price. Do a search on the Internet for "antique flea markets" and see what pops up.

Beyond where you shop, there are other ways to stick to your budget while searching for your wedding gown. The following will give you other ideas to keep in mind:

❤ Pick up the phone before you pick up your car keys. Before rushing to a shop that has a dress you are interested in, give them a phone call. Ask about their prices and their ordering information. You may discover that a gown you are in love with is being discontinued and is being sold at a discounted price. You can easily save money this way.

❤ Always comparison shop. When you are visiting one shop or salon after another, be sure to take note of store policies on alterations, ordering times, refund stipulations, and the shop's overall flexibility. Things to watch for include the quality of dresses, newness of stock, orderliness of the shop, and what types of guarantees offered to you. Take a notebook with you, and do not be afraid to jot down observations, rates, and policies. Later you will be happy you have this information.

❤ When narrowing down choices on the salons and shops you like the most, give the Better Business Bureau a call. You want to find out if there have been any complaints or reports against the shops you are considering. Be sure the shop you do business with has a clean record. You can locate the Better Business Bureau telephone number to call by typing in the appropriate information at its Web site: **http://lookup.bbb.org**.

Here are a few tips to help you shop:

❤ Keep the formality of your wedding in mind as you try on dresses. Although you may fall in love with an ultra formal gown, if you are having a casual wedding, it will not be appropriate — and your guests may feel underdressed. Staying within the formality of your wedding will help keep your budget in check.

❤ When you find a gown you love, be sure it is of high quality. Wedding dresses need to stand up to a long day of wear. Inspect the seams and the stitches to be sure the dress is well made so that you do not have a fashion disaster on your wedding day.

❤ Consider purchasing a simple gown. Unless you have your heart set on a beaded gown, avoid them, as the extra work it takes to create the beaded look raises the price. Even if you absolutely must have a beaded dress, there are ways to get the look you want and still save money. Purchase a simple gown and the pearls/beads you want separately. If you are handy with a needle and thread, stitch them on yourself. If that thought petrifies you, hire a seamstress to do it. You will still save money.

❤ Look at the material the gown is made of. By purchasing a dress made of less expensive fabric you can save an incredible amount.

♥ If your wedding is semiformal, informal, or even casual, a shorter dress may be just the ticket. Plus, the price tag will make you smile. There are stunning tea-length dresses available, as well as suit dresses; do not forget them as you browse.

♥ Ask about sample gowns. Many bridal salons sell their sample gowns at incredible savings, so this may be an option for you. Before purchasing one, however, ensure there are no stains or smudges from being tried on so many times by the salon's customers.

♥ Always ask the bridal salon manager when a new shipment of gowns is scheduled to arrive. By knowing ahead of time, you can be one of the first to browse through the new gowns, having the first pick of the inexpensive ones.

The following hints will assist you in every area of shopping for your dress:

♥ Do you have a friend or family member who works in a bridal salon, dress store, or a department store? If so, ask if you can use his or her employee discount to save 10 to 20 percent off your gown.

♥ Do not order your wedding dress before you and your fiancé have set your wedding date. This is a recipe for disaster if you buy a summer gown only to end up with a winter wedding. Either you will have to wear your sleeveless dress in frigid temperatures, or you will lose your deposit money when you cancel the order to place another.

♥ Watch for sales. End-of-season sales, holiday sales, and prom season sales can lead to a beautiful gown at a fraction of the original cost.

♥ When you hit up the sale rack, be sure the sales are actually sales. Sometimes a salon or shop will set a price that is not actually a markdown. This is why you must comparison shop.

♥ Be open and consider dresses marketed as prom dresses, bridesmaid dresses, holiday dresses, and other types of formal gowns. Simply altering your view about your wedding dress can lead you to the perfect gown for a terrific price.

♥ If you find a dress you love priced at the full market price, but it has a tiny flaw — one you can easily fix — ask for a discount. Something as simple as a torn seam can save you $100 or more off the final price. Just be sure it is a flaw that is fixable.

♥ Begin your shopping excursions early in the day so that you will be full of energy and less likely to make a choice out of fatigue.

♥ Get a dress you can wear again. Choose a gown that can be altered to be less formal after your wedding day, so you can wear it again. Whether this means shortening the length of the gown or trimming off some of the embellishments, it is something to consider.

♥ Always use a credit card when paying for your wedding gown, whether the full purchase price or a deposit. You will find it much easier getting a refund, if necessary.

♥ Do not leave a deposit on more than one gown in several different stores. You likely will not receive a refund when you make your final choice; therefore, pay a deposit on the one and only dress you want. Be sure before spending money.

♥ Be organized in case of a disaster or miscommunication by keeping sales slips, specifics of the dress you ordered, the size, the promised date of delivery, and anything else to do with your dress. You may even want to have the sales consultant sign the record for proof.

♥ If you use an in-store seamstress, have your measurements and the recommended dress size recorded on your order form to save a hassle if the wrong size dress comes in.

♥ Alteration fees can add up. Reduce the possibility of last-minute alterations by wearing the bra, slip, and shoes you will be wearing on your wedding day to avoid mishaps. Also, always get receipts for your fittings.

♥ If you must have an expensive gown and you have not been able to find discounts on it, plan ahead. If you have your wedding date set, and you cannot see yourself getting married in any other dress, then accept you will pay a large price for the gown you want. By planning ahead, you can have your dress put on layaway, and you can make payments throughout the months before your wedding.

Top Five Wedding Gown Tips

The following five tips will help you stay on track when you are shopping for your wedding gown:

1. Your dress does not have to come from a wedding salon.

2. Comparison shop over time.

3. Watch for sales and take advantage of the discounts.

4. Get everything in writing and save it all for your records.

5. Stick to your budget, and do not be swayed by an overzealous wedding sales consultant.

You can save considerable money on your wedding gown if you know what you want, where to look, and how to take advantage of all the different resources available. Good luck in finding the wedding dress of your dreams and sticking to your budget. It can be done. After you find it, you will not mind all the hard work and planning because you will be the stunning bride you always wanted to be.

Online Sources — Discount Wedding Gowns

The following Web sites sell discount wedding gowns. Each of these sites carries a large selection at a variety of prices.

- ♥ Angeri — **www.angeri.com**

- ♥ Arnella's Bridal — **www.arnellas.com**

- ♥ Best Bridal Prices — **www.bestbridalprices.com**

- ♥ Dori Anne Veils — **www.dorianneveils.com**

- ♥ House of Brides — **www.houseofbrides.com**

- ♥ NetBride — **www.netbride.com**

- ♥ Pearl's Place — **www.pearlsplace.com**

- ♥ Perfect Bridal — **www.perfectbridal.com**

- ♥ Plus Size Bridals — **www.plussizebridals.com**

- ♥ Priceless Bridals — **www.bargainweddinggowns.com**

- ♥ RK Bridal — **www.rkbridal.com**

- ♥ Stylish Bridal — **www.weddingdressdiscount.com**

- ♥ Sydney's Closet — **www.sydneyscloset.com**

❧ Your Wedding Veil and Headpiece ❧

You have found the wedding dress of your dreams and have stuck to your budget. Now it is time to shop for the perfect veil and headpiece to show off your dress. Wearing a veil on the wedding day is one of the ceremony's most treasured traditions.

The veil has a varied, eclectic history. Ancient Greek and Roman brides wore a veil to block evil spirits. In the days of arranged marriages, a groom did not see his bride's face until after the ceremony was over, when he was finally able to raise the veil. The Christian tradition of a father lowering his daughter's veil before the ceremony and the groom raising it afterward began in England in the 1800s and continues to this day.

If you choose to wear a veil, you have many options available to you. A veil and headpiece can cost as much as $500, and you could end up spending more of your wedding budget on the veil than you did on the gown. At the end of this section, we offer you several ways you can save money on this important accessory.

Before deciding on which type of headpiece and veil you want, you should understand the styles available.

Wedding Veil Styles

♥ **Blusher or Shoulder-length** style is a veil either worn forward over your face or back over the headpiece. The shorter length will easily pull the eye to the bride's face, and therefore gives the bride a softened, romantic appearance. This length of veil can be used in any formality of wedding, but if your dress has an extremely long train, you may want to consider a longer veil.

♥ **Elbow-Length** veils fall to the elbow and are perfect for short dresses without a train. Because of its length, it helps highlight any detailing at the waist of your gown.

♥ **Fly-Away** are veils with multiple layers that just brush the shoulders. This type of veil can be used in any formality of wedding.

♥ **Fingertip Length** veils fall to the fingertips and often have more than one layer. These veils are one of the most popular and can be used for formal and for semiformal ceremonies.

♥ **Ballet or Tea-Length** veils fall to the ankles and make a beautiful addition to both formal and semiformal gowns.

♥ **Chapel Length** veils are the perfect accompaniment to a full-length gown, as they fall to the floor.

♥ **Cathedral Length** veils are the most formal of all veils and often extend six inches to one foot beyond the train of the gown.

Headpiece Styles

♥ **Floral Wreaths** are simply a circle of flowers that rests on top of the bride's head. They may or may not circle at the forehead. They may be worn with a veil or without.

♥ **Juliet Cap** sits at the crown of the head and is encrusted with pearls, sequins, and other beads.

♥ **Pillbox** is a small, round hat that is worn either centered or back on the head, often with blusher-style veils.

♥ **Mantilla** is a large scarf that drapes over the head, secured with an elaborate comb, and gently frames the bride's face. There is no additional veiling used with a mantilla.

♥ **Picture Hat** has a large brim, often elaborately decorated with lace, beads, pearls, and sequins.

♥ **Tiara** is a crown-style headpiece that rests high on top of the head, encrusted with crystals, pearls, lace, and sequins.

♥ **Coronet headpieces** feature a crescent-shaped base that is decorated with satin, silk, and/or lace, resting high on the crown of the head.

When deciding on the right headpiece and veil for you and your wedding gown, keep the following helpful hints in mind:

♥ The veil should frame your face and complement your wedding gown.

♥ Consider having your veil made with a detachable option so you can remove the veiling from the headpiece after the ceremony and photos are completed. You will have an easier time dancing and celebrating.

♥ If there are embellishments on your dress, try to match them to your headpiece and veil.

♥ If your wedding gown is ivory, do not choose a white headpiece and veil. Match the colors as closely as you can.

♥ Consider the fabric, formality, and length of your gown and train when deciding on your headpiece and veil.

♥ Bring a swatch of fabric from your gown whenever you head out to shop for other accessories. White comes in varying shades, as does ivory; be sure you get the closest match possible.

♥ All embellishments add to the weight of the headpiece. Be sure you do not add too much. You want to be as comfortable as possible, and chances are you will wear the headpiece for many hours.

Ways To Save on Your Wedding Headpiece and Veil

There are plenty of cost-saving tips to help you stick to your budget and find a headpiece and veil that you will love. Consider these options:

♥ Comparison shop. As you visit bridal salons and shops, take some time to browse through their sale and discount racks.

♥ Browse bridal discount catalogs to see what savings can be had there.

♥ Renting your veil is another option. If you are not uncomfortable about wearing a previously worn veil and if you are not worried about keeping your veil forever, it is an option to consider.

♥ Wear a family member's veil. Whether your mother's, your grandmother's, or a favorite aunt's, if the style and color match your gown, consider this option.

♥ If you, a friend, or family member is a talented seamstress, you can have your veil and headpiece handmade. Some ideas include using a fabric headband and adding pearls and netting, creating a wreath from fresh or silk flowers and adding lace, or even using a posh little hat that you decorate with embellishments.

♥ There are also easy-to-use veil kits you can make your own veil from, and everything is included. Cost efficient and easy to do make for an irresistible combination.

♥ Consider going without a veil if you are having an informal ceremony. A simple wreath, hat, or other headpiece may be all you need to add the finishing complement to your gown.

♥ Check antique stores. You may find an absolutely stunning headpiece and veil that need little more than cleaning for a great price.

Online Sources — Discount Wedding Veils and Headpieces

The following Web sites sell discount wedding veils and headpieces. Many of the previously listed Web sites for discount wedding gowns will also have a selection of veils and headpieces for sale.

♥ The Bridal World — **www.thebridalworld.com**

♥ Veilubridal — **www.veilubridal.com**

♥ Vision Veils — **www.visionveils.com**

Your Wedding Shoes

Whether you are aiming for the fairy tale princess, the sassy pixie, the chic fashion plate, or something entirely different, finding the right bridal shoes can be a pain, literally and figuratively.

You have been so caught up in finding your wedding gown and wedding veil, you may have overlooked the importance of your wedding day shoes. If you are wearing a floor-length gown, the shoes you choose will not be as important in appearance as a bride with a shorter gown. You want them to be comfortable. All brides, regardless of the formality of their wedding day, want every aspect to be as perfect as possible, but do not forget you will be in these shoes for hours.

You should plan on purchasing your wedding day shoes after you have chosen your gown but before any fittings have taken place. The reasons for this are:

1. You will need a swatch from your gown when selecting your shoes. The colors and fabrics should be as close a match as possible. It is important to realize that unless your shoes are made from the exact same fabric your gown is, you will not get a perfect match. It is better to focus on how closely you can match.

2. All your fittings should be done while you are wearing your bridal shoes. This is because full-length wedding gowns are hemmed to floor length, which means you will need your shoes purchased and on your feet for the alterations to be correct.

Whether you want stained pumps, three-inch heels, or sassy boots, here are some helpful hints to consider when shopping for your shoes:

♥ If you are not accustomed to wearing overly high heels, do not start now. Instead, try a shoe with a low heel. If you truly have your heart set on high heels, buy them early and break them in far ahead of time; otherwise, your feet will pay the price.

♥ When you break in your shoes, begin the process at least a couple of weeks before your wedding, and start by wearing them only for an hour or two. Do this inside only, so you do not end up scuffing the outside of your shoe. As the day gets closer, increase the time you are wearing them so you can be sure that you will be comfortable on your wedding day.

♥ Consider the embellishments on your wedding gown when choosing your shoes, and make sure they coordinate well with each other.

♥ Match your shoes to the fabric at the hem of your dress, rather than the bodice.

❤ Hit the stores at the end of your day, when your feet are at their largest.

❤ Look for shoes in the size, width, and heel height you are comfortable wearing.

❤ When trying on shoes, wear stockings rather than socks. The difference this makes in the fit is enough to carry around a pair of footies or knee-high pantyhose in your purse.

❤ Consider purchasing two pairs of shoes, one for the ceremony and a more comfortable pair, such as ballerina slippers, for the reception. Your feet will thank you.

❤ Consider the height of the groom when deciding on your heel height.

❤ If your dress is full length, your shoes are not going to be seen anyway, so go for comfort unless you need to add height to your frame.

❤ Scuff up the bottom of your shoes to help with traction. Many new shoes are slippery, and the last thing you want is to fall on your behind on your wedding day.

Ways to Save on Your Wedding Shoes

Even a pair of simple white shoes can be inflated in cost simply by being labeled "wedding shoes." You do not have to spend a fortune on your shoes; they are a small accessory to your dress. The following cost-saving tips will help you find ways to save:

❤ Do not order your shoes in a bridal salon or shop. Chances are great that you will pay a considerable amount more than you will in a regular shoe shop. The markup at bridal salons can add $50 or more to the price of your shoes.

♥ Check the Yellow Pages for discount shoe stores in your area and shop there. Of course, you will also want to be sure the shoes you buy are of high quality as well as of good price.

♥ Watch for seasonal shoe sales where you can save a ton. Sometimes you can save 50 percent or more off a pair of shoes, depending on what sales you hit.

♥ Antique stores will likely have absolutely stunning shoes, especially antique lace-up boots, and often at an amazing price.

♥ Factory outlet stores are a great place to check for amazing discounts.

♥ You can always borrow your shoes from a family member or friend who has the same size foot you do. This is an especially great tip if your sister or best friend was married recently, because their shoes are likely sitting in the closet gathering dust.

♥ Buy a wedding skimmer. A skimmer is a slipper-type shoe available in white satin. Affordable and comfortable.

♥ Consider ordering the same style shoes as your bridesmaids will be wearing, so you can take advantage of a group discount. In some cases, your shoes may even be free with a minimum order of other shoes.

♥ Ignore the fancy shoes and select a plain pair. Beads, sewn-in designs, and other embellishments add to the cost.

♥ Consider ballerina slippers for your wedding day shoes, especially appropriate if you are wearing a floor-length gown since your shoes will not be seen. They are light, comfortable, and will see you through the day well. Check dancing supply stores.

♥ If you already have a pair of nice white shoes that are comfortable, consider wearing them. Not only will you save by not purchasing a new pair of shoes, you will not have to spend extra time breaking them in. Just be sure they are in good condition and not scuffed.

♥ If your heart is set on a beautiful but expensive pair of shoes with rhinestones, pearls, or other beadwork on them, buy a plain pair and decorate them yourself. It is easier than it sounds and will save you money. Check out these sites for ideas in decorating your own shoes with rhinestones, ribbons, and jewelry: **www. do-it-yourself-weddings.com/rhinestone-shoe-clips.html** and **www.associatedcontent.com/article/12695/quick_tips_for_ decorating_your_shoes.html.**

♥ Ignore anything labeled as "wedding" or "bridal" shoes. That label comes with a heavier price tag than normal shoes. Enlarge your options and your pocketbook by considering beautiful white leather, metallic silver, metallic gold, and other types of formal shoes that are not classified as "wedding" shoes. Often, these everyday shoes are more comfortable, less money, and equally as attractive.

♥ Do not overlook used shoes. If you have time to comparison shop and find your size, used shoes are a fabulous alternative. Many brides wear their shoes once and then drop them off at a consignment or used bridal store to sell. They should be in great shape, and you can save a considerable amount.

♥ If you are shopping far enough ahead of time, you have the ability to make the best use of all the sales. Wait to buy summer sandals at the end of the season to save.

♥ Purchase a pair of white dyeable shoes and have them dyed to match the gown if it is not pure white. Also, the shoes can be dyed after the ceremony to another color to get more use out of them.

Online Sources — Discount Wedding Shoes

The following Web sites sell discount wedding shoes and ballerina slippers. Each of these sites carries a large selection and a variety of prices:

♥ Capezio Dancewear — **www.capeziorvc.com**

♥ Dancewear Solutions — **www.dancewearsolutions.com**

♥ Discount Bridal Shoes — **www.discountbridalshoes.com**

♥ Discount Wedding Shoes — **www.discountweddingshoes.com**

♥ My Glass Slipper — **www.myglassslipper.com**

Other Bridal Attire Accessories

After you have your wedding gown, headpiece, veil, and shoes, you are almost done. There are a few other accessories to round out your ensemble, such as:

Wedding Gown Undergarments

The undergarments will be a part of your comfort level, and they should be taken into consideration at every fitting.

Your Slip

♥ If possible, do not purchase your slip at a bridal salon. As with every other accessory, the price will be marked up by 30-50 percent, so you will do far better to purchase your slip at a department store or through an outlet store.

♥ Many gowns come with a slip or crinoline built in them at no extra charge. If yours does not, do not pay extra for one at the salon.

♥ Does the wedding gown you have purchased truly need a slip? Check your gown in different lighting indoors and outdoors, direct sunlight, and spotlights to see if you need a slip. If you do not, and you are comfortable, just forgo it.

♥ Many bridal salons rent slips at reasonable prices. Chances are you will never need a slip such as this again, so why not save some money and just rent it?

Your Garter

♥ Tossing the garter is a tradition slowly dying away. Consider forgoing this custom.

♥ If you and your fiancé decide to toss a garter, you may want to purchase two. This way, you can keep the one you wear throughout the ceremony as a memento and toss a cheaper garter during the reception. You can buy these "cheapie" garters in many lingerie stores or make one.

Other Undergarments

♥ Although fancy silk stockings will certainly make you feel beautiful, they tend to be rather expensive. Save your money and buy basic stockings instead. You will be so caught up in the day, you will not even miss them, and you will still feel stunning.

❤ Another reason to stick to the basics in stockings is so you can buy two pairs. Have one pair tucked away in case you need them.

❤ When you choose your stockings, be sure they complement your gown. If your dress is white, do not purchase ivory stockings.

❤ Skip the nonessentials. Gloves, parasols, and the like will take dollars out of your wedding budget and add little to the day.

❤ Rather than buy new lingerie to wear under your wedding gown, use a set you already have, or if your bridesmaids throw you a bridal shower, save a set you receive as a gift to use on your wedding day.

❤ Browse through discount stores, catalogs, or clearance sales for your wedding bra and panties. Check Victoria's Secret for some of its two-for-one sales and other special discounts online at **www.victoriasecret.com.**

❤ If your wedding gown is thick and detailed and if you are small chested, consider going braless. You can also have bra cups sewn into the dress. Chances are you will be more comfortable and you will save that extra expense.

Online Sources — Discount Bridal Attire Accessories

The following Web sites sell various discount bridal attire accessories. Each of these sites carries a large selection at a variety of prices:

❤ Best Bridal Prices — **www.bestbridalprices.com**

❤ Bridal People — **www.bridalpeople.com**

❤ Marilyn's Keepsakes — **www.marilynskeepsakes.com**

♥ My Gowns — **www.mygowns.com**

♥ Under Cover Bridal — **www.undercoverbridal.com**

Your Wedding Day Jewelry

♥ Jewelry for your wedding day is an important accessory. You may want to consider borrowing it from your mother, your grandmother, or another family member. Not only will this fulfill the "something borrowed" tradition, but wearing a treasured piece of jewelry will add another facet of specialness to your day.

♥ If you choose to not borrow jewelry for your wedding day, you may want to hold off purchasing anything. There is a better-than-average chance your fiancé will purchase a piece of fine jewelry as your wedding gift.

♥ If you do decide to purchase jewelry, save some money by considering high-quality costume jewelry. Many boutiques and online shops offer beautiful imitation or man-made gemstones that, without a jeweler's glass, are next to impossible to discern from the real thing.

♥ Keep your jewelry to a minimum. Too many pieces of extravagant jewelry will detract from your budget and also from your wedding photographs.

Online Sources — Discount Wedding Jewelry

The following Web sites sell costume wedding jewelry at a reduced price. Each of these sites carries a large selection at a variety of prices:

♥ All Costume Jewelry — **www.allcostumejewelry.com**

♥ Glam For Less (GFL) — **www.glamforless.com**

♥ Wedding and Bridal Jewelry — **www.weddingandbridaljewelry.com**

♥ Wedding Sparkles — **www.weddingsparkles.com**

⋙ *Final Thoughts* ⋘

Whether you have $300 or $2,000 budgeted for your wedding gown and accessories, you can find the perfect ensemble. The lower your bridal attire budget means more time searching for the best deals, but it can definitely be done.

Your list of priorities should be:

1. Determine your bridal attire budget, including gown and all accessories.

2. Research magazines, the Internet, bridal shops, and bridal shows to decide on your likes and dislikes.

3. Ask questions.

4. Comparison shop.

5. Think creatively.

6. Purchase your wedding gown.

7. Purchase your veil and headpiece.

8. Purchase your shoes before any fittings take place.

9. Round out your purchases with other accessories and jewelry, borrowing if possible.

Although this process may take some time, by following the guidelines in this chapter you will be successful in finding the wedding gown of your dreams.

Before you know it, your wedding day will arrive, and you will be the Princess for a Day as you meet your fiancé at the end of the wedding aisle. On that day, everything you put into locating the right dress will be well worth it, especially when you see the look in your fiancé's eyes as he watches you walk toward him.

6

Attire for the Groom & Wedding Party

Now that you have found your wedding gown, it is time think about the rest of your wedding party. It is up to you and your fiancé to outfit everyone from your bridesmaids to his groomsmen to both of your parents.

The Bridesmaids

The Bridesmaids' Dresses

For many brides, choosing the gowns their bridesmaids will wear is significantly more difficult than selecting their own wedding gown. The size of your bridal party will likely make the process more difficult because with more people come more opinions.

You are in charge of selecting your bridesmaids' gowns. Although they hope for the best, they are expecting the worst. If you have ever been a bridesmaid, you can understand their apprehension. You will need to find a way to remain true to your vision for your ceremony and still keep your bridesmaids as happy as possible. You want to be considerate in the cost of their gowns, because your bridal party will likely pay for their own attire and accessories. Arriving at the appropriate dress for the appropriate cost and keeping everyone happy may not be as difficult as you think.

There are a few things to consider when you begin this process. The bridesmaids' gowns need to complement your gown and the formality of your wedding. Plus, you will need to consider the varying body shapes of each of the women in your bridal party. What may be gorgeous on your sister may look abysmal on your best friend. The same goes for color.

When you are ready to begin the hunt for the bridesmaids' dresses, it is recommended that you either go by yourself, with your maid of honor, or with one bridesmaid only. Do not bring the entire bridal party along until you have narrowed your selection down to two or three styles. Even then, if the styles can be shown via the Internet, go that route for the least fuss.

Before beginning to search, send a basic questionnaire out to each attendant. You should ask each of them these questions:

- ♥ Are any styles taboo?

- ♥ What is your favorite and least favorite color?

- ♥ What is the maximum you want to spend on the dress and the accessories?

- ♥ What are the best days/times available for fittings?

After you have the answers to the above questions, you can begin looking at gowns. Browse bridal magazines, online sources, and bridal shows to get an idea of the current styles and colors. Keep the following in mind:

- ♥ Your bridal party's dresses should complement your wedding gown.

- ♥ Try to find a style and color that will look good on each person in your bridal party. Think about hairstyle, body shape, and coloring.

♥ When is the wedding? Be sure whatever fabric, style, and color choices you select go well with the season.

♥ Have a range of acceptable prices from each member of your bridal party, so that you do not exceed anyone's budget.

♥ How formal is your wedding? If your dress is tea length, you will not want to choose full-length gowns for your girls.

Questions to Ask Bridal Salons about Bridesmaids' Dresses

As you call and visit bridal salons and dress shops, bring along these questions to ask:

♥ Are there designer catalogs available to take home or to be sent to you?

♥ Which designers' gowns do they carry?

♥ Do they have sample gowns to try on? If so, what sizes are they?

♥ Do they have color charts so you can easily see which colors are available with each dress you may be interested in?

♥ Do they have actual swatches of the fabrics on hand for the dresses?

♥ Can you browse through the dresses yourself, or are they hidden in a back room where only a sales consultant can access them?

♥ After a dress is ordered, what is the standard delivery time?

♥ If a dress needs to be received quickly, is rush service available?

♥ Do any discounts apply? This could include a group discount based on the number of gowns being ordered, the fact you ordered your wedding gown there, or even free or reduced alterations and/or accessories.

♥ Do they carry enough dresses within your bridal party's budget range to make it worthwhile to shop there?

Ways to Save — Bridesmaids' Dresses

Even though the bridesmaids' dresses are purchased by your bridesmaids, you should help them save their money. Consider the following:

❤ If you have a smaller bridal party, such as two or three attendants, consider shopping at major department stores. You will find gowns on the racks in your bridesmaids' sizes.

❤ Another reason to consider major department stores is for the price. Also, if you do have a larger bridal party, the department store may be able to check with other locations to find all the sizes you need.

❤ Outlet stores are amazing places to find excellent deals. Most dresses will be 50-60 percent off the normal full price.

❤ Do not forget about trunk sales and sample sales. Even if you did not go that route for your wedding gown, tremendous savings for your bridesmaids can be found — easily 60-70 percent off full price.

❤ Take a day to go to some area antique stores. Although you are unlikely to find matching dresses, you could find complementary gowns at great prices.

❤ The Internet. There are a number of Internet discount salons online that offer many different choices at all budget levels. The great thing is that it does not matter where your bridesmaids live — everyone can "shop" at the same store.

❤ Hire a seamstress for custom-made dresses. Again, by purchasing the materials, each of your girls can save money.

❤ Have your bridal party rent their dresses. As long as you approve of the style and color, this may be a perfect alternative for your bridal party.

There are other ways to save big when shopping for your bridesmaids' dresses. These helpful hints will get everyone thinking.

♥ The gowns do not have to be the same style. Have each member of your bridal party choose the style she likes the best. As long as they come from the same store and can be made in the same color, each gown will complement the others. The added advantage is that each bridesmaid can choose whatever fits her body shape and budget.

♥ If your bridal party is large and you are shopping at a bridal salon, ask for group discounts.

♥ Consider prom dresses and party dresses, especially if you hit the racks immediately after prom season.

♥ Try to find a style that your bridesmaids will be able to wear again. If a dress can be worn many times, the price tag will not be as hefty.

♥ Look for simpler styles. Just as with your wedding gown, the simpler styles tend to cost less than embellished and/or detailed dresses.

♥ Try to locate bridal shops and department stores that offer free or reduced alterations to save a bundle all around.

♥ For the bride whose bridal party lives all around the country, ask each of them to have their measurements taken professionally. After each does, have her send you the measurements via e-mail or regular mail so you can take the sizes with you when you shop.

♥ All gowns should come from the same store, whether online or off. Do not let your bridesmaids order their gowns from different stores. The colors may not match.

♥ If you have purchased the gowns and need to send them to your far-away bridesmaids, send them priority mail insured and tracked.

♥ You may choose the color, the fabric, and a seamstress. Each of the bridal party arranges to meet with the seamstress and selects her own style to be custom made. By using the exact same fabric, you will have the exact color on each dress, but each will also be unique.

Online Sources — The Bridesmaids Dress

In addition to the online sources mentioned in the wedding gown section, the following Web sites offer great deals on bridesmaids' dresses:

- ♥ Bridal Sassique — **www.bridalsassique.com**

- ♥ Brides and Prom — **www.bridesandprom.com**

- ♥ Chadwick's — **www.chadwicks.com**

- ♥ CyberGown — **www.cybergown.com**

- ♥ Cybernet Plaza — **www.cybernetplaza.com**

- ♥ Glamour Closet — **www.glamourcloset.com**

- ♥ Jessica London — **www.jessicalondon.com**

The Bridesmaids' Accessories

There are ways to save on the remainder of your bridesmaids' attire accessories, from shoes to headpieces to slips to gloves. Share these tips:

Your Bridesmaids' Shoes

Many of the ways you saved money on your bridal shoes can be used by your bridal party. All your bridal party shoes should be ordered from the same store to be sure the colors are an exact match.

- ♥ Consider shopping at shoe stores for your bridesmaids' shoes. They have a great selection and are likely to offer more discounts than a bridal shop.

- ♥ Watch for sales. This is especially true after seasonal holidays, when most sales are at their deepest.

- ♥ Comparison shop. Check out several different stores to be sure you are getting the best price.

♥ Ask about group discounts. You will want to speak with the store manager before choosing the store your bridal party should visit.

♥ Check the Internet. As long as each bridesmaid orders from the same shop, using the same item number, each may save money.

♥ They can wear their own shoes. Most women have a wide variety of shoes in their closet. They should match the gown and be of similar color and style.

Your Bridesmaids' Headpieces

Your bridesmaids do not have to wear headpieces of any sort to be a beautiful complement to you on your wedding day. If you wish for your bridal party to wear headpieces, consider these hints:

♥ Visit a florist and pick up some fresh baby's breath. Your bridesmaids can decorate their hairstyles simply by adding wisps of baby's breath to their upswept hairstyles or using combs.

♥ Make their headpieces or have them make them. You can use a bow with a little netting, decorative combs, floral sprays, or anything else that will add a simple but elegant decoration.

♥ Purchase silk or fresh flowers and ribbon that match the bridal party dresses. Tie one or two of the flowers with the ribbon on the side or the back of their heads.

♥ Sometimes hats make the perfect accessories. You can easily find inexpensive hats and embellish them with ribbons, flowers, or fabric for the perfect touch.

Other Accessories

♥ Most women have an appropriate slip that will work with almost any dress. If your bridesmaids' dresses do not require a special full slip, they should wear one they already own.

♥ If a special slip is needed, your bridesmaids can either rent one, watch for sales, or purchase it at a discount when they buy their dress.

♥ Depending on the formality of your wedding, you may decide to forgo gloves for your bridal party.

♥ If you do wish your bridesmaids to wear gloves, they will be able to find inexpensive ones at department stores. Bridal salon gloves are likely overpriced, so that would be their last alternative.

The Flower Girls

You may have one or more flower girls in your ceremony. Although their parents will purchase their dress and accessories, you can help them save.

The Flower Girls' Dresses

♥ Suggest an inexpensive style that the girls will be able to wear again.

♥ If they already have several party dresses or a First Communion dress, consider letting them wear one of them. Your flower girls do not need to match the bridal party exactly. As long as they are attired in the proper formality dress for your ceremony, almost anything is appropriate.

♥ If a party dress is used, it can be embellished to complement your wedding style and colors. Have a piece of fabric in the same color as the bridesmaids' dresses made into a sash to tie around the girls' waist. You can also add beading or lace to dress up a simpler gown.

♥ Browse through children's discount stores for your flower girls' gowns. Not only will you find an excellent variety of party dresses meant for young girls, but you are likely to find amazing savings.

♥ Check the after-Easter sales at children's dress shops. This is the best time to locate great deals on wedding whites and pastels.

♥ Have the dresses made by a family member or friend who is a seamstress, or hire a seamstress. You will be able to choose the exact style you want and the fabric you want, and it will be custom made to your flower girls. Do not do this too far ahead of time, however, because children's sizes change rapidly.

The Flower Girls' Accessories

Here are some tips for any of your flower girls' accessories:

Their Shoes

♥ If your flower girls already have party shoes, they can use those and save their parents' money.

♥ Consider ballet slippers for your flower girls. They are affordable, comfortable, and charming.

♥ Skip purchasing flower girl shoes at bridal salons. They will absolutely be overpriced. Instead, visit department stores or national chain stores to get the best deals.

Their Headpieces

♥ A simple wreath of flowers will be precious.

♥ Incorporate ribbons and flowers into a long braid down the side or back of your flower girls' heads if they have long hair.

♥ Use a comb or bobby pins to sprinkle baby's breath, or another small flower, throughout their hair for a sweet, pretty look.

Their Baskets

♥ Appropriate baskets can be found at craft stores, discount stores, on the Internet, or right after Easter.

♥ Tie a matching piece of ribbon around the handle of the basket into a bow to complement your other colors.

Online Sources — Flower Girl Dresses

The following Web sites sell flower girl dresses at a reduced price. Each of these sites carries a large selection at a variety of prices.

♥ Girls Dresses — **www.girlsdresses.com**

♥ Little Girl Dresses — **www.littlegirldresses.com**

♥ So Sweet Boutique — **www.sosweetboutique.com**

♥ Water Lily Kids — **www.waterlilykids.com**

Your Mother, Your Fiancé's Mother

Although it is not your obligation to purchase the dresses your mothers will wear, you may want to help your mother and your fiancé's mother in their selection. Since there will be family wedding photographs taken, you may want to steer them toward complementary colors and styles. Also, they will appreciate your assistance in helping them save money.

The Mothers' Dresses

You will want to meet with your mother and your fiancé's mother either separately or at once. Consider hosting a brunch or a lunch and discussing the attire for your wedding. When you do, bring along some magazines to discuss dresses and colors. By doing this, you will not have to accompany them when they shop for their dresses unless you want to, and you will not have to worry that their choices will be inappropriate.

Things to Think About

♥ The mothers' dresses should complement the formality of your ceremony. If your bridesmaids are wearing tea-length gowns, the mothers' gowns should not be full length.

❤ The mothers' dresses should not outdo your gown, so they should be somewhat conservative in style.

Ways to Save — The Mothers' Dresses

❤ Stay away from bridal salons, as the price will be much higher than non-specialized fine dress shops. Instead, they should look in the dress section of department stores.

❤ Mothers' dresses can be found at a significant savings at major department stores immediately after seasonal holidays.

❤ Outlet stores can also lead to amazing discounts on name-brand designer dresses.

❤ Simple gowns can be made more formal by adding a jeweled neckline, fancy trim, or beads as embellishment.

❤ If your mother or your fiancé's mother lives far away from you, help her by sending her the information she needs: a swatch from the gown the other mother purchased, color ideas, style ideas, and the formality of the wedding.

❤ Check the Internet for discount online shops that offer beautiful dresses at a fraction of the price.

❤ If each has an appropriate dress of the right color and length in her wardrobe already, she should feel comfortable wearing that.

Online Sources — The Mothers' Dresses

The following Web sites sell mothers' dresses at a reduced price. Each of these sites carries a large selection and a variety of prices.

❤ Arnella's Bridal — **www.arnellas.com**

♥ Bridal Discounters — **www.bridaldiscounters.com**

♥ Discount Dresses Online — **www.discountdressesonline.com**

♥ Sydney's Closet — **www.sydneyscloset.com**

⋙ Men's Attire ⋘

All the information you need about your groom, his groomsmen, and the fathers of the bride and groom is given to you here. Men in the wedding are responsible for purchasing, or renting, their own attire.

Tuxedos or Suits

Just as with your gown and the dresses of your bridal party, the men's attire should conform to the location, style, and formality of the wedding. If your wedding is semiformal or informal, a tuxedo is not necessary. Your groom may choose to wear a suit, and this is completely fine.

When deciding on whether to wear a tuxedo or a suit, considering the time of day is also important. Evening ceremonies tend to feel more formal, while morning and early afternoon ceremonies are less so. If your groom decides on a suit rather than a tuxedo, all men in the wedding should look uniform so they stand out from the male guests who may also be wearing suits.

Some ideas for suits

♥ If all the men in the wedding already own their own suits, be sure they are all the same shade. If they are not the exact same color, that is fine as long as they are all dark, or light, or pinstriped.

♥ Consider khaki or tan-colored slacks and a dark blue suit jacket with matching ties. This is an excellent way to coordinate the men without spending a fortune.

♥ All men should wear identical ties. If they are wearing their own suits, a tie would be their only expense.

❤ If the men in the wedding are wearing their own suits, be sure they all fit appropriately and complement each other.

Choosing the Tuxedo

If you and your fiancé decide to forgo the suit in favor of tuxedos, your first step will be deciding what type of tuxedo will best suit the ceremony and your fiancé.

The following chart will assist your fiancé in narrowing down his choices.

Tuxedo Types	Comments on Style
Double-Breasted	A double-breasted jacket can effectively camouflage a larger-sized groom or groomsman. Things to look for: make sure the size is correct, and try on several different cuts/styles to find the right one.
Cutaway	This is the traditional morning coat. The swallowtail lines on the cutaway will be attractive on almost any frame. This is an excellent choice if the groomsmen are of varied heights and body shapes.
High Vest	This style works best on men who are not broad in their upper torso. For men who are broad in this area but want this style, the vest should be in a muted shade for the best look. If your groom is fit, he can do anything he wants with patterns and colors.
Low Vest	Low vests are attractive on almost all body types. Just as with the high vest, broad men should go for muted shades, while fit men can be freer with patterns and colors.
Mandarin/Banded Collar	For men with a thicker, shorter neck, this collar will not work well. A lay-down collar would be a better choice.
Peaked Lapel	The peaked tuxedo lapel is a great choice for shorter men, as it will make the body appear longer because it draws the eye up and out, creating length. This is also a good choice for taller men.
Shawl Collar	Shawl collars come in a variety of widths, and this makes them difficult to adhere to a certain body shape. Pay attention to the width and to the lines of the tux itself and just try your eye.

Tuxedo Types	Comments on Style
Single-Breasted (one- or two-button)	This is the most classic of all tux jackets and will look terrific on most body shapes. Taller men should go for a two-button jacket, while shorter men should go for the one-button. The more shirt that shows means a longer visual line, so shorter men should use that style to add the appearance of height.
Single-Breasted (two- or three-button)	This is a popular jacket. These high-buttoning jackets are amazing on tall, slender men. Heavier men should consider the one- or two-button version.
Tails	This is about as formal as a tuxedo gets. Unfortunately, this style can be unflattering on short or heavy men. It depends on the length of their legs, since even short men can look great in tails — as long as they have height to carry them off.

Those bridal magazines you bought when looking for your wedding gown will be useful for your fiancé when he is deciding on tuxedos. When you find a few favorites, hold the pictures next to a picture of your gown and your bridesmaids' gowns to be sure they complement each other.

Most men decide to rent their tuxedo rather than purchasing one, unless there are several events over the next year that will require a tuxedo. Otherwise, the most money is saved by renting a tuxedo.

Ways to Save — The Tuxedo

Even though the groomsmen and the fathers pay for their own tuxedos, whether renting or purchasing, you can still help them save money. Consider the following when searching for tuxedos for your wedding party:

♥ Ask for tuxedo rental recommendations from family and friends who were recently married. You will be able to learn about prices, reliability of the business, and quality of the tuxedos.

♥ Check your Yellow Pages for area rental companies and then compare prices. You may be surprised at how much they can differ.

♥ Ask about group discounts, especially if you have a large wedding party. Sometimes, the groom will receive his rental at no charge.

♥ If you do find a shop that offers the groom a free tuxedo based on the group rental discount, find out if that savings can be passed on to one of the fathers or split between the two.

♥ To save money on extra fittings, be sure to acquire professional measurements from any of the men who live out of state. They should have their measurements taken at a professional tailor for the most accuracy.

♥ Get a signed copy of the contract, order receipt, and any other papers that will detail the style numbers, delivery dates, deposit amount, check number, and the name of the clerk who helped you if a mistake is made, because you will be able to prove all necessary information.

Shoes for the Men

Many men already have a pair of black dress shoes in their closet. If this is the case, they can use the ones they already have. Other thoughts are:

♥ Most tuxedo rental shops rent shoes at a discounted rate for the entire male wedding party. Be sure the one you choose offers this option.

♥ Watch for sales and discounts at major department stores.

♥ Check the Internet and the Yellow Pages for discount shoe outlets.

Your Ring Bearers

If your wedding ceremony includes a ring bearer, the following helpful hints will save money for his parents:

♥ If the ring bearer will be renting a tuxedo, be sure to see if a discount applies at the rental shop the rest of the men are using.

♥ Even at formal weddings, ring bearers can wear a suit and be absolutely dashing. If your ring bearer already owns an appropriate suit, just let him wear that.

♥ Shoes can be rented from the tuxedo rental shop. Ask about discounts.

♥ Alternately, shoes can be purchased from children's shoe stores. Watch for sales to get the best deals.

♥ Ring bearer pillows can cost anywhere from $60 to more than $200. Save your money and craft your own. See this Web site for the how to: **www.thriftyfun.com/tf746562.tip.html**.

♥ If you do not have the time or skills to make a pillow, borrow one from family members or friends who were recently married.

♥ Even ring bearer pillows go on sale. Watch for discounts and sales, especially from bridal outlet stores.

Online Sources — Ring Bearer Attire

♥ Advantage Bridal — **www.advantagebridal.com/ribeandcoat.html**

♥ Dapper Lads — **www.dapperlads.com**

♥ Dressed Up Kids — **www.dressedupkids.com**

♥ Little Girls Dresses — **www.littlegirlsdresses.com**

Final Thoughts

Dressing your wedding party can be tiresome, frustrating, and time consuming, but it can also be fun. When you have this portion of your wedding planning complete, you will be excited, because it will be easier for you to envision the ceremony. You have myriad details left to work out, but you should definitely pat yourself on the back for getting this far.

Invitations, Thank You Cards, and More

Your wedding budget can take a huge hit depending on the decisions you make for your invitations, response cards, thank you cards, programs, and other types of written communication. Paper and ink can add up to quite a hefty total when each of these areas is combined. The average cost a couple pays for all the stationery needs related to their wedding, assuming 150 guests, is more than $500. You can spend less than this, or you can spend more.

This chapter helps you sort through all the information and gives you tips on how you can save money on wedding stationery.

Your Wedding Invitations

The invitations you and your fiancé send will give your guests their first indication of what to expect at your wedding. The thickness of paper, the printing, and the way the invitation is worded will speak volumes for your ceremony.

You will be able to find the perfect style to suit your wedding, regardless of how formal or informal it is. The first step is to know what decisions you need to make.

The Traditional Wedding Invitation

The traditional wedding invitation is often on white or ecru stationery. It is oversized, engraved, and on heavy paper with a see-through tissue overlay and an inner envelope, which is sent inside an outer envelope. Within the invitation, a response card, a reception card, and a map/direction card are also enclosed. Sometimes, additional cards are also included with the invitation.

If your wedding is formal, you will want to consider the traditional wedding invitation, as it is pure elegance.

Today's Wedding Invitation

Although the traditional wedding invitation will never go out of style, there are other alternatives. Some of them will save you money.

Thermography Instead of Engraving

About 20 years ago, a printing process called thermography became an option for wedding invitations. Until this time, engraving was the only option, and as engraving can be pricey, thermography gave many budget-minded brides an attractive alternative.

It mimics engraved printing but costs less. It is available in different colored inks to customize the appearance of your invitation.

Just as with engraving, thermographed invitations offer a raised print on the front. The difference between the two is small and not worth the extra cost for engraving. Invitations printed with thermography do not have the tell-tale indentation on the back of the invitation as engraved invitations do. Even if your budget is not limited, you can save money with this option.

Lettering and Inking Styles

When you are ready to order your invitations, you will need to select ink colors. If you are on a tight budget, stick with black ink, as there will be no extra charge. Colored ink will raise the price of your invitations slightly.

Many companies also offer a type of ink called foil-stamped ink. Although this ink is shiny and that may appeal to you, it costs more. Many invitations are hard to read when printed in foil-stamped ink, so you should ask to see a sample before you select it.

Your invitation catalog will also have several pages with examples of lettering styles. Available styles will range from plain to fancier script-style fonts. Pay close attention to the examples, because some fonts will appear too dark in black ink, in which case you may want to pay the extra for colored ink.

The best advice is to look at actual sample invitations and not just the individual letters on the sample page.

Styles of Envelopes

Traditionally, invitations are sent with an inner and an outer envelope. If you are not concerned with having an inner envelope, it is perfectly acceptable not to have it.

If you do choose to have an inner envelope, one of your options will be to have a lining. You will be able to choose from different linings, and depending on your choice, the cost will vary. You can always choose a plain envelope without a lining to save a little.

You should consider paying the extra money to have your return address printed on the envelope. You can also have your address printed on the response cards. Although it does cost extra, this one simple step will save you hours of hand-writing your address.

The Parts of a Wedding Invitation

Invitations may have inserts you can include, if you wish. The following will describe each insert and give you suggestions for them:

Response Cards

Response cards are simply small cards with at least two lines of text. Some ask for a specification regarding the reception and a meal preference. If a guest is able to attend the ceremony only, this information will be of help to your caterer. Other times, when there is more than one meal choice, the caterer will need to know how many of your guests will be eating prime rib and how many will be eating chicken.

The response card will have a preaddressed and pre-stamped envelope so that all your guests need to do is mark the appropriate boxes and mail it.

Maps/Direction Cards

If you intend on sending out maps/direction cards, you may add them to your invitation package, as it will be easier for your guests to have everything arrive at once.

You can draw your own map, or you can create one on your computer. You do not have to use fancy paper or be extra creative. The point of the map or direction card is clear and concise directions. You do not have to be an artist to create it.

Permanent Address Cards

Permanent address cards are often inserted into the wedding invitations. Their purpose is to give your guests the address of your home after you are married. It can include your telephone number. You can print this information on your wedding programs or provide it when you send thank you cards after the ceremony.

You can either print this information off on your computer or order business cards with your new information on it. Business cards are small, so they will fit in an invitation or a thank you card easily, and they will cost you almost nothing to get. By using a source such as **www.vistaprint.com**, you can receive 250 business cards for free. You will have to pay postage, but that is only a few dollars.

❧ Where to Buy Invitations ☙

Just as there are countless styles of wedding invitations, there are countless retailers who sell wedding invitations, online and off. The following retail sources will give you an idea of where to start shopping:

♥ Stationery shops are plentiful. To find ones in your area, just look under "invitations" or "wedding invitations" in the Yellow Pages.

♥ The Internet. You can order your invitations right from your computer. It is recommended to request samples before doing so, however, to be sure of the quality you will receive. If you are in a hurry, this will likely be your fastest choice.

♥ Mail-order catalogs. When you look through your wedding magazines, you will see advertisements for all kinds of wedding vendors, including mail-order companies that specialize in wedding invitations. Call their toll-free numbers, and they will send you their newest catalog and possibly samples. Many of these companies allow you to order online, so you will not even have to pay for postage to mail your order.

♥ Discount printers. Discount buying services sell the same premium brand names that exist in the stationery stores but at a reduced price. They do not have any catalogs, so you will need to know what you want when you call. You can find their telephone numbers in wedding magazines, online, and sometimes in the Yellow Pages.

Shopping for Invitations — Things to Know

When you begin searching through shops, catalogs, and the Internet, keep the following thoughts in mind:

♥ Your invitations should reflect the formality of your wedding, from the ceremony to the reception. When considering the styles, stationery, and lettering you like the most, do not forget to match them up with your vision for your wedding.

♥ Before you start to shop, know how many invitations you will need to order. This will allow you to compare deals.

♥ The amount of money you have dedicated to invitations should also include your postal costs. Couples can easily overspend on invitations when they forget to add in the cost of postage. You may require three first-class stamps per invitation, two for mailing the invitation and one for the response card. If your invitation is large, you may need more. Take one to the post office to check, before ordring postage.

♥ If you are perusing invitation mail catalogs, do not forget the price of shipping and handling in your final tabulations.

♥ When you find the perfect invitation, you may be tempted to order it immediately. Be aware that by ordering too early, you could face a problem if there is a last-minute change of date, time, or place. Four to six months in advance of your wedding is an appropriate time to order your invitations.

Placing Your Order — Things to Know

The following hints will help you stay clear of the most common mistakes:

♥ Order 10-15 invitations to use in case of returned invitations, additions to the guest list, and misaddressed envelopes. Any leftovers can be used as mementos.

♥ When going through your guest list to arrive at an accurate count, follow these guidelines: one invitation per family at the same address, except when there are children over the age of 18, as they should have their own. If you are inviting someone who is bringing a guest, add the guest's name. There is no need for two invitations.

♥ Proofread your order form carefully. Mistakes can cost a bundle when you try to rectify them later. You should also have at least two other people read through it to see if they catch anything you missed.

- ❤ Read the contract before placing the final order to see what the supplier's policy on returns is. You want to ascertain that if the supplier makes a mistake in the printing or if there is damage during shipping, the invitations will be reprinted and reshipped at no additional charge to you.

- ❤ All receipts, contracts, and a copy of the order form should be kept in your files. It is a good idea to take note of the salesperson's name, in case there is a problem later. Record the date of your order, details about the style and the amount of invitations you ordered, any changes that you may make, delivery information, amount of deposit, and any further payment obligations. All this will help you have a point of reference in the event of a mishap or error.

- ❤ It may seem like good money sense to skip out on ordering response cards with your invitations, but it is not. Response cards are the easiest way for you to know who is coming to your wedding. Although you may save a few bucks by not ordering them, you will have less stress and frustration in the long run by ordering them.

Receiving Your Order — What to Check

When you receive your wedding invitations, you will be excited. Even so, try to quell your excitement long enough to be thorough in going through them. You will want to do the following:

- ❤ Review them carefully. The sooner you find any mistakes, the more likely you can get them corrected.

- ❤ It may be time consuming, but go over each invitation separately. Just because the top ten are perfect does not mean there is not a problem. You want to look for smudges, off-center printing, and stationery issues, such as rips and tears.

- ❤ Count them. Be sure you actually received the number of invitations you ordered.

♥ Check your final invoice to be sure no additional charges were added on without your knowledge. If there is anything you do not understand, compare it against your original receipt and contract. If you find a discrepancy that should not be there, find out how to be compensated.

Mailing Your Wedding Invitations

Here are a few pointers when you are ready to mail your invitations:

♥ Be sure to mail your wedding invitations early enough so your response cards can be returned in time to give your caterer a final head count. Delays in notifying your caterer will likely cost you additional money.

♥ Go through the guest list and ascertain that all the addresses you have listed are still correct. If an invitation is returned to you, you have wasted postage and possibly hurt someone's feelings.

♥ To save time, check out the U.S. Postal Service's Web site at **www. usps.com**. You can order certain stamps for your invitations, look up zip codes you may not be sure about, and double-check postage rates.

Ways to Save — Your Wedding Invitations

Before purchasing your wedding invitations, be sure to go through the following list:

♥ Comparison shop in all sources of wedding invitations. This includes stationery stores, catalogs, and Internet sources.

♥ Give yourself sufficient time to shop. The worst decisions are often made in a hurry.

♥ The simpler the invitation, the less it will cost. Choose plain black-and-white invitations instead of the fancier types. Extras such as colored ink, pictures, borders, monograms, and laser-cut designs will inflate the price. Simple does not mean unattractive.

♥ Choose thermography over engraved invitations for a considerable savings, up to 50 percent.

♥ Skip the colored envelopes with shiny liners in favor of the less expensive, plain variety.

♥ Watch the size of your invitations. The larger the invitation, the more you will pay in stationery and postage costs. Smaller invitations can be just as classy and elegant as their larger counterparts.

♥ Purchase an embosser with your return address instead of having it printed on your envelopes. Although the price will be about the same, you will be able to use the embosser for many years. Check these office supply stores for prices:

    ♥ Green Light Office — **www.greenlightoffice.com**

    ♥ Living Victorian — **www.livingvictorian.com/embosserhome. html**

    ♥ Office Depot — **www.officedepot.com**

    ♥ StampCo — **www.stampco.com**

    ♥ Staples — **www.staples.com**

♥ Choose a stock of stationery that is thin and less costly. Heavier weight does not necessarily equal better invitations.

♥ Order all your stationery needs at the same time. Many suppliers and printers offer a discount based on quantity ordered. Think about thank you cards, response cards (RSVP cards), wedding programs, and any other need you may have.

♥ Instead of using a response card, which requires an additional envelope and a first-class stamp, consider using a postcard, which will save money on postage. You can even print them yourself.

♥ Consider purchasing your invitations from a warehouse club, such as Costco (**www.costco.com**). It offers name-brand invitations with a savings of 10-30 percent.

♥ If you have a high-quality computer and printer at home, consider printing your own wedding invitations. You can purchase your own cardstock, paper, and envelopes at any stationery store, or you can purchase wedding invitation kits that come complete with templates and clip art. If you are making your own invitations, a few Web sites to check are:

  ♥ Envelopements — **www.envelopements.com**

  ♥ LCI Paper — **www.lcipaper.com**

  ♥ Formal-Invitations.com — **www.formal-invitations.com**

  ♥ My Gatsby — **www.mygatsby.com**

  ♥ Wedding Clipart — **www.weddingclipart.com**

♥ Another alternative is to design your own invitations and then take the design to a discount printer or office needs store, such as Kinko's, and have them print or copy as many as you need. This alternative will likely be more expensive than printing them yourself, but it will be less pricey than a professional printer. It will also save you time, a valuable commodity when you are planning a wedding.

♥ If there is a local community college with a graphic arts or other arts program, it may offer discount services on designing and printing. Call the college to see if it offers a program such as this. If so, you can get professional-quality invitations at a fraction of the cost.

♥ If you or a friend or family member is talented with calligraphy, you can have a master copy made and then have copies printed, or if there is time and willingness, each invitation can be hand-written using calligraphy.

❤ If you like the idea of calligraphy for your invitations but do not know anyone with the talent, check local college art departments and find out if there are any students with a talent for calligraphy. If so, you may be able to hire them to make your master copy.

Sources for Wedding Invitations

From mail catalogs to online sources, you can find what you need without ever leaving your home.

Mail Order Catalogs for Wedding Invitations

You can get catalogs from these vendors:

CATALOG NAME	WEB SITE ADDRESS	PHONE NUMBER
American Stationery Co	www.americanstationery.com	800-822-2577
The American Wedding Album	www.theamericanwedding.com	800-428-0379
Anna Griffin Invitations	www.annagriffin.com	888-817-8170
Ann's Bridal Bargains	www.annsbridalbargains.com	800-821-7011
Heart Thoughts	www.heart-thoughts.com	800-648-5781
Invitations by Dawn	www.invitationsbydawn.com	800-361-1974
Jean M	www.myjeanm.com	800-766-8595
Now & Forever	www.now-and-forever.com	800-521-0584
Precious Collection	www.preciouscollection.com	800-635-3898
Reaves Engraving	www.reavesengraving.com	877-610-4499
Rexcraft	www.rexcraft.com	800-635-3898
Willow Tree Lane	www.willowtreelane.com	800-219-1022

Prices vary per supplier, so be sure to comparison shop.

Online Sources — Wedding Invitations

Here are some other invitation suppliers you can access via your computer. Although most of these are discount suppliers, some are not:

- ♥ Botanical Paper Works — **www.botanicalpaperworks.com**

- ♥ Crane & Co — **www.crane.com**

- ♥ Custom Shots Photo Invitations — **www.customshots.com**

- ♥ eInvite — **www.einvite.com**

- ♥ Elegant Brides Invitations — **www.elegantbrides.invitations.com**

- ♥ Embossed Graphics — **www.embossedgraphics.com**

- ♥ Fine Stationery — **www.finestationery.com**

- ♥ Invitation Hotline — **www.invitationhotline.com**

- ♥ Invitations 4 Less — **www.invitations4less.com**

- ♥ Invitations 4 Sale — **www.invitations4sale.com**

- ♥ Invitations by Karina — **www.invitationsbykarina.com**

- ♥ Julie Holcomb Printers — **www.julieholcombprinters.com**

- ♥ Let's Party by Jake — **www.letspartybyjake418.com**

- ♥ PaperStyle.com — **www.paperstyle.com**

- ♥ Sand Scripts — **www.sandscripts.com**

- ♥ You're the Bride — **www.yourethebride.com**

- ♥ Wedding Invitations 411 — **www.weddinginvitations411.com**

❧ Other Wedding Stationery ❧

Beyond your invitations, response cards, permanent address cards, and map/direction cards, there are other types of stationery you may decide you want for your wedding.

Wedding Programs

Wedding programs are a little extra that can add something special to your wedding day. A wedding program is primarily a record of your wedding ceremony, letting guests know what to expect. It also introduces your wedding party to them, and it will be a beautiful memento.

Consider having a wedding program if your ceremony meets the following criteria:

1. If your ceremony is religious and you are having many guests who are of another faith

2. If your ceremony is traditional and you are having many guests who are of another culture

3. If your wedding is large and many of your guests will not know the wedding party

4. If your ceremony is long and you want your guests to be able to follow along

5. If you have many people you would like to thank

Before you decide if you want a wedding program or not, it may help to understand what makes up a wedding program:

- ♥ **The Cover** will include the date and you and your fiancé's names. You can also include a picture or design, the location, and the time of the ceremony.

- ♥ **The Order of Events** will detail what will happen during the ceremony, including:

  - ♥ Processional Music

  - ♥ Greeting

  - ♥ Readings

  - ♥ Prayers

  - ♥ Exchange of Vows

  - ♥ Ring Ceremony

  - ♥ Any other ceremony, such as Unity Candle Ceremony

  - ♥ Pronouncement of Marriage

  - ♥ Recessional Music

  - ♥ Any other details, such as soloists, other music, and the like that are unique to your ceremony.

- ♥ **Members of the Wedding Party**, including the officiant.

You may wish to include other specifics in your wedding program, such as:

- ♥ An explanation of any rituals or traditions in your ceremony.

- ♥ Requests for guest participation in certain sections of your ceremony, such as kneeling or singing.

- ♥ Any people you wish to thank.

- ♥ A short bio about each member of your wedding party, no more than a sentence or two for each.

- ♥ An explanation for your choice of location, a certain song, etc.

♥   Verses about love or marriage.

♥   Directions to the reception.

Wedding programs can be ordered from a printer, or you can make your own on your computer. If you choose to make your own, you can either print them yourself or print one master and have copies made. If you choose to have a wedding program at your ceremony, you do not have to spend much money on it.

Place Cards for Your Reception

You can have your place cards printed at the same time you have your wedding invitations printed. This is especially true if you are receiving a discount for ordering a quantity of stationery. Other options include printing them yourself on plain white or a matching color to your wedding cardstock.

Saving money on place cards is the same as on any part of your stationery. Comparison shop, look for discounts, and consider printing them yourself. Also, place cards are not a necessity, so determine if you need them.

You can order decorative place cards for both scenarios. Here are a few sites to look at:

♥   Place Cards.com — **www.placecards.com**

♥   Cambridge Paper — **www.cambridgepaper.com**

♥   Documents and Designs — **www.documentsanddesigns.com**

You also have many choices in how you display your place cards at the reception. Place card holders come in a variety of sizes and shapes. They cover all types of themes, and can be elegant, fun, simple, or extravagant. Here are a few sites to view that offer discount place card holders:

♥   Wedding Accessories — **www.weddingaccessories.net/plachold.htm**

- ♥ Wedding Things — **www.weddingthings.com/wedding_placecard_holders.htm**

- ♥ Wholesale Place Card Holders — **www.easelmoments.com**

Thank You Cards

You can order thank you cards when you order your invitations if you are getting a discount for ordering in quantity. Consider the following:

- ♥ Purchase plain white thank you cards from a discount retailer or a department store. They do not need to be wedding thank you cards.

- ♥ You can also purchase high-quality stationery and hand-write your thank you in black ink.

- ♥ Do not simply print out mass thank you notes from your computer, as this is considered tacky. Your thank you notes should be written by you and your fiancé.

⇨ Final Thoughts ⇦

Stationery costs can take a bite out of your wedding budget if you do not plan ahead, comparison shop, and scale down where necessary. There are many ways you can save big on your invitations, response cards, thank you cards, and any other stationery needs.

Wedding Day Flowers

The colors and aromas of fresh flowers add a natural beauty that little else does. If having flowers at your wedding is important to you, you will find money-saving ideas in this chapter.

The average cost of flowers for a wedding depends on the city in which you live. They usually cost about 20 percent of your budget. However, lavish affairs can make the price five times that. You can also spend far less. Regardless of your floral budget, you can have beautiful flowers at your wedding.

There are three categories of wedding day flowers to consider before you start shopping:

1. **Personal Wedding Flowers** — Personal flowers for your wedding party include the bride's bouquet; bridesmaids' bouquets; boutonnieres for the groom, the groomsmen, and the fathers; corsages for the mothers; petals for the flower girl to toss; and a boutonniere for the ring bearer.

2. **Wedding Ceremony Flowers** — You may want to decorate the site of your ceremony. Flowers may decorate the altar and pews.

3. **Wedding Reception Flowers** — You can have as many or as few flowers as you want at your reception. Things to consider include the guest tables, the gift table, and the cake table.

In addition to the above, you may also require flowers for your rehearsal dinner. If you are unsure of what you will need for your flowers, the following worksheet may help narrow your requirements:

✺ Wedding Flower Worksheet ✺

Bridal Party Flowers	Qty	Personal Wedding Flowers	Qty
Bride's Bouquet		Mothers' Corsages	
Maid of Honor Bouquet		Grandmothers' Corsages	
Bridesmaids' Bouquets		Godmothers' Corsages	
Flower Girls' Flowers		Aunts' Corsages	
Groom's Boutonniere		Other Corsages	
Best Man's Boutonniere		Fathers' Boutonnieres	
Groomsmen's Boutonnieres		Grandfathers' Boutonnieres	
Ushers' Boutonnieres		Uncles' Boutonnieres	
Ring Bearer's Boutonniere		Other Boutonnieres	

Flowers at Ceremony	Qty	Flowers at Reception	Qty
Pew Bows (for church)		Cake	
Altar Flowers		Cake Table	
Candelabra		Main Table	
Aisle Flowers		Guest Tables	
Outside Arrangements		Guest Book Table	
Door Arrangement		Gift Table	
Other		Bride's Tossing Bouquet	

✺ Lilies and Roses ✺

After you know how many flowers you need, think of the type of flowers you want. There are far more types of beautiful flowers than could possibly be listed here, so it is impossible to give you a complete guide. However, the two most common flowers in wedding bouquets are roses and lilies.

Roses are Red

Roses are, by far, the most popular wedding day flower and with good reason. They are considered a symbol of timeless beauty, romance, and love. When shopping for roses, you should know they come in three main varieties:

1. **Hybrid Tea Roses** are the classic rose most commonly thought of for weddings. Uniform in appearance, this commercial rose is the bud you are most likely to see in a florist shop.

2. **Spray Roses** have a natural, garden-grown look, with five to ten small heads on each stem.

3. **Garden Roses** have busy, open heads and are the old-fashioned variety, often costing more money.

Many brides believe that "bridal white" roses are pure white. This is not true. Some bridal roses have a white hue and when carried in a bouquet tend to have a pinkish color. The following rose colors will help you know what to expect:

❤ Bridal Pink roses are a mellow, but not pale, pink.

❤ Candia roses have dark pink edges on their creamy white petals.

❤ Champagne roses are a creamy antique white that often look pale pink.

❤ Darling roses are a creamy white with a peach hue.

❤ Delores roses have a creamy pink hue.

❤ French Anna roses are large, creamy in color, with pink tips.

♥ Jacaranda roses range from a dark red to a hot pink.

♥ Jacqueline Kennedy roses are a true red with a smaller bud.

♥ Lady Diana roses are pale peach and at times pinkish.

♥ Madame Delbard roses are a rich, velvety red.

♥ Passion roses are a dark, rich lavender.

♥ Prelude roses are pale to medium lavender.

♥ Sterling Silver roses are a silvery pale lavender.

♥ Tineke roses are pure white. This is the most popular white rose for brides.

The Beauty of the Lily

Lilies symbolize purity, chastity, and innocence, making them popular for weddings. Most flowers in the lily family have ornamental flowers often described as showy and pendulous. There are many types of lilies, but these are the most commonly used for weddings:

♥ Calla Lily, also known as the "arum" lily, is an elegant, trumpet-like blossom. This large, long flower seems to burst from its straight, thick stalk. Calla lilies are available in creamy white, yellow, orange, pink, and purple.

♥ Lily of the Valley has bell-shaped florets that dangle from a slender stem and has a fresh scent. It is available in white and in rosy pink, though the pink is much rarer.

♥ Rubrum Lily is a breathtaking star-shaped flower often used in bridal bouquets. It comes in shades of white, peach, and purple.

Other Popular Wedding Blooms

The following is a list of other popular flowers used often in weddings:

- ♥ Gardenias exhibit a heavy sultry scent and have creamy ivory petals.

- ♥ Hydrangeas come in intense shades of pink, blue, burgundy, and purple.

- ♥ Peonies have large, full heads with a strong scent and bright color.

- ♥ Ranunculus is a rose copycat that looks the same but costs less.

- ♥ Stephanotis is traditionally used in weddings because of its meaning, "marital happiness." The blooms are star shaped and grow on a flowering vine.

- ♥ Sweet Peas signify lasting pleasure and are a delicate bloom with a candy-like scent.

- ♥ Tulips represent consuming love and "happily ever after" and are grown in a myriad of colors.

Inexpensive blooms can fill out your arrangements and decrease your overall flower cost. The most popular inexpensive flowers are ivy, gerbera daisies, zinnias, Queen Anne's lace, and leatherleaf. Tulips are also a low cost alternative.

Floral Tips

When you are considering what kind of flowers, types of bouquets, and the floral decorations for your wedding, the following advice will come in handy for you:

- ♥ The shape of the bridal bouquet should fit the height and size of the bride. A short bride will look hidden behind a big bouquet. If you are tall, consider carrying a cascading bouquet. If you are short, avoid cascading bouquets, unless they are smaller.

♥ Smaller, more sculptural bouquets are more in fashion for weddings than ever before. Brides like the nosegay or hand-tied bouquets, as they are small enough to not cover up the detailing of their gowns.

♥ Your bridesmaids' bouquets should be smaller and more colorful than your bouquet. Your maid of honor's bouquet should be smaller than your bouquet but slightly larger than the bridesmaids'.

♥ If the place of your ceremony has high ceilings, the altar flowers should be tall.

♥ If your ceremony is at night, white flowers will add light in the shadows, while dark flowers will get lost in the shadows.

♥ Your bouquet should complement your gown and the formality of your wedding.

♥ Climate can affect flowers. If climate is a concern, choose sturdier flowers rather than fragile ones.

♥ Your flowers and colors in your bouquet should reflect your personal style.

♥ A common mistake is for a bride to choose many different colors within her bouquet, rather than a theme.

➣ Finding a Florist ➣

When you begin shopping for flowers, you will find there are three basic types of florists.

1. You will see cash-and-carry florists in places like your grocery store. They specialize in those quick arrangements you need for Mother's Day, Valentine's Day, and birthdays. Best Bet: Small, informal

weddings where many flowers are not necessary.

2. Full-service florists handle everything from weddings to wire service arrangements to other special events. Most florists are full service, though, as in any business, some are better than others. Best bet: small to midsize, informal, or semiformal weddings.

3. Specialists are florists who focus on one or two specific areas, such as weddings and corporate affairs. Best bet: any type of wedding, but if your wedding is large or formal, you may want to consider a wedding floral specialist.

Questions to Ask Florists

As you begin investigating florists in your area, be ready with a list of questions to help narrow down your choices.

❤ Are examples available? Ask to see examples of their work, both in photographs of past weddings or special events and live examples.

❤ Do they require a deposit to hold your wedding date? If so, what is their deposit and refund policy? You do not want to be surprised by any fees.

❤ Do they charge a delivery or setup fee? Some florists include the delivery fee in the cost of the flowers, while others tack it on at the end.

❤ How many weddings do they schedule per day? Many florists handle several weddings in one day. You will want to choose a florist who will dedicate its day or some of its staff to your wedding and your wedding only.

❤ Do they offer silk or dried flower arrangements? If so, are they available for rent? You may want to consider a mix of fresh, silk, or dried flowers for your wedding and ceremony to save money.

♥ Do they offer any rental items? If so, what is the cost? This could include arches, ferns, or even other wedding necessities such as tables and chairs.

♥ Ask if you can attend one of their weddings during the setup, so you can see whether the florist is organized and dependable.

♥ How far in advance do they normally arrive at the ceremony and reception sites to set up? Setting up can take a while, especially if the ceremony and reception are being held in two different locations. Your florist should arrive two or three hours ahead of time.

♥ Will they simply drop the flowers off at the sites, or will they spend time making sure everything is in order?

♥ Will they give you a written proposal that specifies the exact flowers and costs? When you get a proposal, be sure that each item you need is priced individually, so that you know the real costs.

♥ Do they preserve bouquets? If you have decided to preserve your wedding bouquet, find out whether they can handle that for you.

What to Bring to the Florist Meeting

When you have narrowed your choices to two or three florists, you will want to set up an appointment to meet with them. While there, you will want to pay attention to the shop, the cordiality of the staff, and how comfortable you feel. In addition, you will want to bring the following with you:

♥ Note cards with the time of the wedding, the location of the wedding, and any restrictions that your ceremony and reception site may have regarding decorations and flowers.

♥ A photo of your wedding gown and the bridesmaids' dresses.

- ♥ A swatch of fabric from your wedding gown and from the bridesmaids' dresses.

- ♥ Magazine photos of flowers and bouquets that you like.

The florist will also need to know the color scheme of your wedding. Be sure to tell the staff if you have any floral allergies. You do not want to sneeze or have watery eyes throughout your ceremony and reception.

Wedding Flowers on a Budget

Wedding flower costs can reach into the thousands, but they do not have to. The following section will give you ideas on saving your money so you can meet your budget.

Ways to Save — Wedding Flowers

The first step to saving money on your wedding flowers is in the florist you choose. Consider these tips before selecting your florist:

- ♥ Avoid the fancier florists you will see connected to bridal salons, hotels, and malls. Their prices will be elevated to pay for their premium location. Moderate suppliers will have better rates.

- ♥ If your family has a regular florist, put it on your list to visit. You are already familiar with it, its level of service, and its dependability. Because you are a regular customer, you may receive a discount.

- ♥ Shops that grow most of their flowers and plants on site will be less expensive than shops that order everything.

- ♥ Visit with floral wholesalers in your locality for discount prices. You can find them in the Yellow Pages.

- ♥ Ask friends and relatives if they can recommend a florist.

♥ Look for new businesses that are hungry to gain a good reputation. Although these beginners may have less experience, they have plenty of talent, and their prices will likely reflect their need to attract new business.

When deciding on the arrangements and the types of flowers, keep these following tips in mind:

♥ Order flowers that will be in season when you have your ceremony. Prices are higher for out-of-season blooms.

♥ Compare prices for each of the flowers you are interested in before making a choice. Your florist should have a chart to show you the prices, what has to be flown in, and the availability of each.

♥ Consider a mix of cheaper blooms surrounding a few pricier flowers as the center of attention. In this way, you can have gorgeous arrangements at a fraction of the cost.

♥ Consider agreeing to a "market buy." Florists can take advantage of wholesalers' deep discounts on their weekly sales. Although you will not know what your flowers will be until the week of your wedding, you can save money this way.

♥ Popular flowers, such as carnations and baby roses, are often priced less. If you like them, plan your arrangements around them.

♥ If your wedding is in a popular month, forgo the traditional blooms. They include white roses, stephanotis, and gardenias. The demand will be higher and so will the cost.

♥ Miniature flowers are more delicate than their full-sized counterparts, and they also cost less.

♥ Adding a few sprays in your bouquets will save money. You get several flowers per sprig to give a fuller appearance to your arrangements.

❤ You do not need to order an exact replica of your bouquet as your tossing bouquet. It should be smaller with far fewer flowers in it.

❤ Many florists give the tossing bouquet at a discount or even free to the bride. Ask if your florist does this.

Budget-minded brides will love these ideas for decorating the ceremony and the reception:

❤ Instead of paying a fee for the rose petals for the flower girl, gently pull the petals off roses from your garden. If you do not have a garden, find out who in your wedding party does.

❤ For winter weddings that fall directly after Christmas, cut off evergreens from your tree or purchase a tree at a discount after the holiday.

❤ Borrow potted plants from friends and family. They are free and will add to the décor.

❤ Move the altar arrangement to the reception from the ceremony. One decoration will get double duty to help your budget.

❤ Use your tossing bouquet as a decoration on the guest book table until you need it.

Other tips to consider:

❤ Check with your ceremony and reception location to see if they have silk or dried flower arrangements you can use. You may be able to bypass ordering fresh flowers for decorations if they do.

❤ If your ceremony location is having several weddings on the same day, find out if you can contact the other brides. You may be able to split the cost of decorating the ceremony.

❤ Corsages for the mothers and grandmothers should not be large. Small corsages cost less and are attractive.

♥ Order flowers through a wholesaler and arrange them yourself. If this thought scares you, call your local high schools and community colleges. Any school with a horticulture program will have students ready to arrange your flowers for you for a low fee or even for free.

♥ If your florist charges a delivery fee, ask some friends to pick up the flowers for you. Just be sure you have plenty of insulated coolers and heavy boxes to ensure the flowers stay fresh and uncrushed.

Online Sources — Wedding Flowers

Check out these resources on the Internet for your wedding day blooms:

♥ Fifty Flowers — **www.fiftyflowers.com**

♥ Flower Sales — **www.flowersales.com**

♥ Globalrose — **www.globalrose.com**

♥ Online Wholesale Flowers — **www.onlinewholesaleflowers.com**

♥ Silk Flowers Plus — **www.silkflowersplus.com**

♥ Sommer Flowers — **www.sommerflowers.com**

Final Thoughts

The flowers you choose for your wedding will help create the ambience, the romance, and the style of your day. Take your time when selecting your florist and your flowers, and be sure to communicate exactly what you want.

You can find beautiful flowers for your wedding, regardless of your budget. With a little creativity and the appropriate preparation, every bride can have a breathtaking wedding filled with flowers — without breaking the bank.

Decorations and Accents

Decorations are not just about flowers. Although flowers can add a special beauty to your wedding and reception location, you have other choices for decorating if your floral budget is low. Even if you have exactly the flowers you want, you can accent their beauty and add to your wedding day décor by using candles, lights, bows, and even balloons.

Decorations will help set the scene for your special day. With your imagination, a little time, and a small amount of effort, you can transform your ceremony and reception into a perfect reflection of you and your fiancé's personalities, tastes, and the special magic that makes you a couple.

Unfortunately, wedding decorations can take up a significant portion of the wedding budget. To some degree, the decorations you choose will largely depend on where your wedding ceremony and reception are located, the formality of your wedding, and even the amount of guests that will be in attendance. Obviously, small, informal weddings will cost less to decorate than large, formal affairs. Regardless of your wedding and your budget, you can save money.

Your Wedding Ceremony Decorations

The decorations you choose for your ceremony will largely depend on where the ceremony is. From places of worship to the beach, your choices will vary.

Place of Worship

Most wedding ceremonies are held in a place of worship. If this is the case with your wedding, you are already one step ahead in the decorating process, as many churches, synagogues, and the like have beautiful architectural details built into them. Stained glass windows, rich wooden pews, breathtaking altars, and high ceilings will give you a tremendous starting point in decorating. All you will need are a few accents to pull everything together.

Before purchasing or renting any decorations, consult with the officiant or the church office to find out about any limitations. Some places of worship prefer no candles or flowers, while others are open to these types of decorations. After you know what your ceremony location allows, you can begin to plan the ambiance of your wedding.

Altar Decorations

Many brides make the mistake of too heavily decorating the altar area of the church. This is not necessary, as you, your fiancé, and your wedding party will be the center of attention during the ceremony. The beautiful wedding gown you have purchased will be the focal point. With this in mind, you should keep your altar decorations to the basics.

If flowers are allowed, consider simply going with two sprays to add color. If flowers are not allowed but candles are, two candelabras will set the mood just fine. It is also perfectly acceptable to use both.

For ceremonies in which neither flowers nor candles are acceptable, consider using tulle to decorate columns and the podium. You can easily make a few beautiful swags to add a little extra pizzazz for your ceremony.

Altar Railings

Altar railings are another place to add some swags of tulle, which can be done inexpensively, especially if you make them yourself. Another idea is to twist ivy throughout the railing to add a touch of green.

If your budget is exceptionally tight, however, this is one place you can skip the decoration completely. Most of the guests will not even notice the altar railings.

Candelabras

Often, churches will have several tall floor candelabras made of brass or copper that you can use at no charge. This is a way to save some money, as you can use them as an alternative to flower sprays. Purchase candles that match your ceremony for a personal touch. If you have extra fabric from your bridesmaids' gowns or can purchase a similar fabric, you can make bows for the candelabras. Simple bows with a bit of greenery will attract the eye and add a beautiful accent.

Unity Candles

If you and your fiancé decide to use a unity candle, you do not have to spend $35 or more on one. There is no reason to purchase a candle labeled as a unity candle for the sentiment to be exactly the same. Purchase a normal candle in a height and color you like, add some flowers or greenery around the base, and you have a unity candle for far less money.

The Church Pews

As your guests enter the church and look down the aisle, their eyes will take in the full beauty of their surroundings. Because the aisle is the center of the church, adding some decoration to the pews can help you achieve the look you want.

Pew Bows

Pew bows are one of easiest and least expensive decorations you can add to your wedding, and, because the pews are so visible, they will definitely add to the overall décor. To save money on pew bows, make the bows yourself. The following ideas will get you started:

♥ Brocade bows are perfect for formal weddings. Brocade is a heavier fabric, rich in feel and in look.

♥ Patterned bows, whether floral, plaid, checked, or other types of patterns, are for more casual weddings. If your wedding is informal, being held outside, or is a spring or summer ceremony, floral patterns are a beautiful way to accent your ceremony.

♥ Tulle is a light and airy fabric that can be used in all types of weddings, any time of year.

♥ Silk, or silk-like fabrics, add a formal touch to all styles of weddings and come in a rich variety of hues, from the palest of pale to deeper shades.

Three yards is a good length of fabric to use per bow, but you should experiment to see what you and your fiancé like the most. Bows can also be adorned with flowers, beads, lace, or greenery.

Pew Candles

Evening and winter wedding ceremonies will make the best use of candles; however, if you have your heart set on them, use them. Candles add romantic light to almost any setting.

Aisle Runners

Aisle runners are one of the unnecessary expenses you can dispose of if you choose. Photographers have found that a bride in her wedding gown does not show up as well when photographed on an aisle runner because the gown tends to blend in with the white of the runner.

Many brides still want to use an aisle runner because of tradition and formality. Check with your church before renting one, as many churches have runners than can be borrowed at no additional cost.

Wedding Ceremony Decorations — Alternate Locations

Today, more and more wedding ceremonies are being held in places other than churches, synagogues, and the like. If your wedding is not in a place of worship, the location will dictate what you need to do for decorations.

For example, if your wedding is outside, such as at the beach, you do not need much in the way of decoration. You have the sand, the surf, and the crashing of waves as your ambience. If your ceremony is in a garden gazebo, you already have flowers and the gazebo to draw attention. For outdoor weddings, the goal is to create a focal point — the place that you and your fiancé will be taking your vows. Some ideas are:

- ❤ Rent an arch and decorate it with flowers, greenery, ribbons, and/or bows to add to the affect.

- ❤ Use potted plants and flowers to create a spectacular focal point for your ceremony.

- ❤ Rent a gazebo and decorate it with flowers, greenery, ribbons, bows, and/or balloons.

- ❤ Rent a tent for you and your guests. You will never need tents of such size again, so you definitely want to rent, rather than purchase.

- ❤ There are rental places all over the country. One of them, Taylor Rental, a nationwide rental service, has many of the supplies you would need for an outdoor wedding, including tents, arches, and more. Visit **www.taylorrental.com/catalog.asp?cat_id=11**.

If your wedding is indoors, you can still rent an arch or create another focal point for you and your fiancé to take your vows. Potted plants and flowers work just as well inside as they do outside. Be creative. The goal, for both the indoor and the outdoor ceremony, is a beautiful place for you and your fiancé. It can be as simple or as elaborate as you like.

Some ideas for decorating the rest of your ceremony include:

♥ Make your own bows, as described above, but attach them to the outside chairs that frame the "aisle" you will be walking down.

♥ An aisle runner, while still not necessary, may make more sense in a location that is not in a place of worship. It will help to distinguish the ceremony location and will lead to the focal point of the ceremony.

♥ Balloons can be used to add festivity to your ceremony.

♥ Plants, whether real or artificial, will bring in some natural color.

♥ For indoor weddings, decorate the entrance of the house, room, or building with a wreath, potted plants, balloons, or a combination of all three to signify that something special is going to happen.

Your Wedding Reception Decorations

When your guests enter the reception location, the first thing they will see is the entrance. Take a little time to plan out what decorations you would like to use here, as it is the first impression of the rest of your wedding day.

♥ An arch of balloons makes a beautiful and celebratory entry. If you are not too picky about the arch itself, you can make your own. Be sure you have something to weigh down each side of the arch, and use a frame made out of cardboard, wire, or anything else that will give you a sturdy base. Tie, staple or wrap your balloons around the frame as tightly as you can.

♥ For a simpler approach with balloons, just have them floating in the room, with ribbon streamers trailing down. This is especially dramatic over the dance floor.

♥ Potted plants are also a terrific way to mark the entrance of your reception. This is especially true if you wrap lights, such as twinkle lights, and bows throughout to make a dazzling presentation.

♥ For evening weddings, a table on each side of the entry filled with candles makes a glowing entry. Be sure to clear it with the locale.

♥ Bring in small trees to add warmth to the location.

♥ Tulle or netting can be used in a variety of ways to add to your décor. Consider pooling it on tables, draping it over chairs, or even hanging it from the ceiling in an ethereal cascade to add a romantic touch.

♥ Make bows to put on the backs of chairs, hang on doorknobs, or artfully place on the corners of each table.

Other areas you will want to decorate at your reception include:

The Cake Table and the Gift Table

You should have a table set aside where guests can place their wedding gifts. Although you do not necessarily have to decorate this table, it is an easy way to add some inexpensive flair and color to the room. Some ideas are:

♥ A tablecloth that drapes to the floor in either white or a color that coordinates with your wedding.

♥ A basket that can be placed in the center for guests' cards.

♥ Your tossing bouquet could be set on this table as a center decoration until it is time for you to throw it.

❤ Ribbons and bows along the sides of the table in an alternate color to the tablecloth

Your cake table will be one of the centerpieces of your reception, so you should spend some time thinking of appropriate accents to show off your wedding cake. In addition, you do not want a plain wall behind the cake, as this is the backdrop for any cake photographs. Some ideas are:

❤ Cover the cake table in a white or ivory floor-length tablecloth. Tablecloths do not have to cost much money. Watch for sales at department stores, especially after holidays, to get incredible deals.

❤ For added appeal, add a secondary tablecloth, in a coordinating color to your wedding motif, gathered up in three or four places around the table. When cinched with bows, this is a beautiful look.

❤ Although you can add other decorations to the cake table, it is not necessary. Your cake is the decoration.

❤ Pull the cake away from the wall a bit and add a spray or an arch behind it.

❤ The arch can be of flowers, greenery, balloons, or a mix of all three — whichever best fits your budget and likes.

❤ A backdrop idea is a lattice screen on which you can interweave greenery, ribbons, and/or bows that coordinate with your wedding.

Guest Table Centerpieces

Centerpieces for your reception can not only add to the décor, but they can also be almost anything. Flowers are an ideal centerpiece, but there are so many more things you can do. Some budget-friendly ideas are:

❤ Was your ceremony at the beach? Have your centerpieces reflect this by filling fishbowls with seashells, starfish, and colorful rocks.

❤ Framed photos of family and friends can take center stage. Just arrange a cluster of different sizes of framed pictures in the center of each table.

❤ Or fill those frames with pictures of you and your fiancé. It is your wedding, and your guests will love seeing your relationship blossom through your photographs.

❤ Pick up some inexpensive glass or clear plastic bowls and fill them with a variety of colorful fruit. For summer weddings, choose tropical fruits, such as limes and pineapples. For winter weddings, deep red cranberries and oranges would look beautiful.

❤ Give your guests a decoration to snack on. A selection of breads, of all different sizes, shapes, colors, and types, is one idea to consider. If you go this route, mix it up so no bread bowl is exactly the same.

❤ Have wedding favors and mementos be your centerpieces. Arrange them on each table so there is enough for each guest seated there. If you will buy mementos anyway, you can get double use out of them.

❤ If you are getting married near a holiday, fill bowls with holiday mementos. For Christmas, you could purchase boxes of inexpensive wedding ornaments. For Easter, eggs decorated in your wedding colors. For Thanksgiving, you can fill baskets with small gourds and pumpkins. Be creative.

❤ Purchase discount glass bottles in different shades, from green to clear to amber, and fill each one with just one or two long-stemmed flowers. Dried flowers work well for this, too.

❤ Candles are a popular centerpiece. See the following section for information on candles for your wedding and reception.

Your centerpieces can be anything you want them to be. By using a little creativity, you can have unique centerpieces without breaking your budget.

❧ The Beauty of Candles ❧

Using candles is a terrific way to save money and to add a special ambience that little else can. The flickering lights, the glow, the warmth, and the romanticism that burning candles offer may make them your number one choice for this special day. If you are on a budget, you can spend little for a tremendous effect.

Many reception venues no longer allow candles due to fire code laws, but if yours does, candles may give you exactly what you want.

Here are some ideas:

♥ Purchase votive or tapered candles for less than a dollar apiece and sometimes, several for a single dollar. An added benefit is that candles come in every color of the rainbow.

♥ Purchase a flat mirror in either a square or a circular shape to place in the center of each table, and then scatter votive candles on the top for a terrific, yet inexpensive, decoration. Factory Direct Craft Supply has some mirrors exactly for this purpose at affordable prices, **www.factorydirectcraft.com/catalog/index.php?cPath=1174**.

♥ Floating candles can be used for another spectacular accent. Consider choosing scented candles to add an additional element to your reception. Use a simple clear bowl, or wide and short vase, and use one to four floating candles per bowl.

♥ If you like to paint, pick up some small pottery bowls or pots, add your creative flair, and then fill them with votive candles. Leave one, or several, at each table. If you want, you can also use this as a memento, and make one for each guest to take home.

♥ Many reception venues and caterers will provide silver candelabras at low to no cost to their clients. If you are able to take advantage of this, you will need to supply only the candles. It pays to check before renting your candelabras.

❤ Inexpensive votive candles in holders of different heights make a stunning presentation.

❤ Tapered candles, or even tea light candles, surrounding a vase with a single flower, are also an inexpensive method to add to the ambience of your reception.

❤ Make a visit to a discount glassware store, flea market, or antique store, and pick up some mismatched wineglasses, water goblets, and other types of glasses to use as votive holders.

❧ Other Ways to Add Light ❧

If your ceremony and/or reception locale do not allow lit candles, you do have other methods of creating the light you want.

❤ Every type of candle in existence also comes in a battery-operated version. Although more expensive than regular candles, battery-operated ones will give you the same ambience and can still be found at decent prices. One place to check is Terry's Village, **www. terrysvillage.com**. There are many vendors who sell these types of candles; just do a search on the Internet.

❤ Use twinkle lights around the room to give a festive glow. You can purchase these directly after Christmas at a tremendous discount or ask your family and friends to borrow theirs. Most people have Christmas lights, and if you label each strand with the person's name you are borrowing them from, you will have no problems returning them after your wedding.

❤ Colored lights, overhead lights, and even spotlights can add excitement to your celebration. Check with your reception locale to see what types of lighting it offers.

❤ For a fun look if your wedding ceremony and/or reception is outside, consider using paper lanterns.

Ways to Save on Decorating

Along with what has already been mentioned, here are some wedding decorating budget tips:

- ❤ Focus your money on where the most attention will be focused — the cake table, the altar, and other places that draw attention.

- ❤ Instead of decorating every pew, decorate every other one.

- ❤ Skip the large floral arrangements for decoration, and instead purchase or rent shrubs, trees, and plants. It will cost far less.

- ❤ Make your own centerpieces.

- ❤ Decide on the essentials first. If you have any budget money left after those are taken care of, then worry about the extras.

- ❤ Artificial flowers may cost you less money for centerpieces and other areas in which natural flowers are not necessary.

- ❤ Make tissue-paper roses to scatter along the cake and gift tables.

- ❤ Visit your dollar store to see if you can get what you need in the form of candles, vases, and other small decorating accents.

- ❤ Minimal décor can be classy. Keep it light and save money.

- ❤ Greenery adds a dash of beauty without being overly pricey.

Final Thoughts

Let your creativity shine when planning the décor for your wedding ceremony and reception. You will not only save money, but you will also end up with a unique, dazzling, and absolutely beautiful ceremony and reception. Have fun!

CASE STUDY: CELEBRATIONS

What is your area of expertise?

Our retail store offers wedding and bridal accessories, invitations, party supplies, balloons, decorations, and more. We specialize in full-service wedding and event décor, featuring both balloon and non-balloon décor. We also have a large variety of rental décor items for the do-it-yourself brides.

What are the most common mistakes you see that result in the bride and groom going over budget?

Oftentimes the couple plans to do as much as they can themselves, which is a good idea, if it's done right. The couple usually starts out purchasing anything they think they may use to decorate their wedding without having a plan or knowing what they truly need. They usually end up spending a lot more money than they realize because it is bought in bits and pieces over a period of time. The other problem is that they end up with a bunch of stuff that doesn't coordinate or work well together, and then they buy even more. Instead of purchasing things to decorate with they would be better off renting these items. Then they will not waste all their time, gas, and energy searching the entire state for more centerpieces or whatever they think they need. They also don't consider the fact that they have to store these items, decorate with them, take them down, clean them, and store them again. Simply renting those items can eliminate all of this hassle.

The other mistake some couples make is using more than one decorator for their wedding. They think they will save money because the other decorator may offer something for a few dollars less. They need to look at the whole picture. If two different decorators are being used for the same event, oftentimes it will be obvious. Each decorator will have a style, and those styles may not work well together. The same concept applies when you try to do parts of the décor yourself. When we provide full service décor for a wedding, the couple always gets more than they paid for. We always bring extra linens, centerpieces, balloons, arrangements, etc. and use these to fill in any areas that may have been overlooked. If there is more than one decorator, the chances of this happening are slim.

Many people think they will save money if they order everything from the Internet. Sometimes this is true, but oftentimes it is not. Once you add shipping and handling to the order, you may end up paying more than you would at a local retail store. You should also consider how much it will cost you to return the item if you are not satisfied with it. In comparison, when you purchase items from a retail store, you can usually see the item in person before you buy it. And most stores will accept returns with no additional expense.

CASE STUDY: CELEBRATIONS

The final common mistake couples make is assuming. For example, our business is a small independently owned store in a small town. Many people assume that our prices will be much higher than the bigger chain stores or even the Internet or mail order. This is true regarding some items. However, the majority of our merchandise is actually priced lower than those alternatives. We see a lot of people price shopping; most of them return to our store and tell us they can't believe we have lower prices than the chain store in the larger city. The other benefit of shopping in the independent stores like ours is the excellent customer service you will receive. We take the time to help you find what you need and offer suggestions to make your event a success. We are experts in the event industry; the chain stores cannot compete with our knowledge or customer service.

If you could offer one piece of advice to a couple planning their own wedding under a budget, what would it be?

Many decorators and wedding planners offer free consultations; take advantage of this and see exactly what they have to offer you. You may be surprised to find they can actually save you money, as well as time and stress. Many couples are afraid to tell wedding professionals what their budget is; they fear the vendors will take every last penny. Quite the opposite is true. By letting us know what your budget is we can help you stay within that budget and make sure you get the most for your money.

What are overlooked areas of savings?

Balloons! Balloons give you the biggest bang for your buck. They quickly fill large spaces with your colors. When used appropriately they can create any atmosphere you wish to achieve. They can be elegant, fun, unique, romantic, modern, sophisticated, and beautiful. It is very important to choose a professional balloon decorator for this service; there's more to it than just blowing up a balloon. Beautiful balloon décor starts with high-quality balloons…. Yes, there is a difference. Proper sizing and equipment is also very important. For help finding a professional balloon decorator in your area you can visit **www.qualatex.com** or **www.balloonhq.com**. Both of these Web sites are excellent resources for balloon décor.

How do a bride and groom stay on budget?

Know your budget and be willing to tell the vendors you are working with what that budget is. You should know what your total wedding budget is and what percent of that budget will be allocated to each area of your wedding. I ask every client I meet with what their budget is, and each time the reply I receive is, "We don't really have a budget" or "I don't know." I oftentimes get the feeling that they do know but just don't want to share that information. If you tell me what kind

CASE STUDY: CELEBRATIONS

of budget I have to work with I will be able to offer décor options that fit your budget. Your decorator should be willing to offer you suggestions and solutions for staying on budget.

You should also determine what is most important to you. For example, if you want your guests to dance the night away and have a good time, you should put more emphasis (and money) on the dance floor and perhaps less in the centerpieces. Your decorator will be able to help you make these decisions, but you need to let us know what is most and least important to you and what your budget is.

How can a couple find quality services at the best price?

Word of mouth is our best advertiser. Ask your family and friends whom they would recommend. You should also ask other wedding vendors for recommendations. Many vendors can steer you in the right direction; they have probably seen the work of many decorators. The next step is meeting with each of the decorators. They should have a portfolio that shows their style of decorating; make sure your styles match. Also make sure the photos they are showing you are of the work they have actually done. Ask for references and check them.

What shouldn't the bride and groom do to cut costs?

I have seen couples decide not to send thank you notes to their guests in an effort to save money on postage and stationery. They put a card at each table thanking guests for attending and giving a gift. This is incredibly rude and was not well received by the guests. You should always send a personal thank you note for each gift you receive.

It's easy to become overwhelmed when planning a wedding. What is your advice for lowering the stress?

Start planning early. Open a checking account specifically for wedding expenses and start saving. You should save pictures of things you love, as well as things you don't like. Showing these pictures to your wedding vendors will help them get a good idea of what you want and don't want as well as your style. Get a binder or expandable file and designate an area for each aspect of your wedding and a place for each vendor. Use a calendar to help you keep track of payments that need to be made and appointments. Keep track of all your expenses, and keep all your receipts and contracts filed appropriately. Don't try to do everything yourself.

Remember, you may actually save money by hiring a wedding consultant…and you will definitely reduce your stress level. A good wedding consultant will also

CASE STUDY: CELEBRATIONS

be able to help you deal with difficult family members or friends by offering solutions to your problems. If you are working with experienced and reputable wedding vendors you will not need to worry so much about everything being perfect. It is their job to make sure everything is perfect.

How would a couple know when a price is truly "too good to be true"?

If the price is much lower than the competitor's it should throw up a red flag. You need to carefully research that company and make sure it has the experience and ability to complete the job correctly. Ask for references and call those references. You need to carefully read the contract for any hidden costs. You also need to be sure the prices you are comparing are for comparable products or services. For example, one decorator may be quoting a price that includes using expensive fabrics like satin or organza while the other decorator is using tulle. You should also make sure that the pictures and portfolio you are being shown are actually the work of your decorator. Some inexperienced decorators will take photos from the Internet, publications, and even purchase photos of other decorators' work and call it their own. This is illegal, and I would suggest looking for another decorator. However, it is acceptable to show photos of work they have not done to give you ideas. They should always tell you that it is not their work but that they can do something similar. This is where your research is important. Make sure the photos of their work reflect the skill and quality needed to recreate the other photos.

Any other suggestions or advice you would like to share?

The one factor that affects the price of nearly every aspect of your wedding is the number of people involved, both guests and your bridal party. The number of guests you invite will drive up the cost of the catering, table linens and chair covers, centerpieces, favors, cake, invitations and thank you notes, postage, the size of the banquet hall, tables and chairs, etc. The size of your bridal party will drive up the cost of flowers and attendant gifts. Reducing the size of your guest list and your bridal party can significantly lower the cost of your wedding or allow you to splurge in other areas.

Tammy Corzine

Celebrations

249 N. Main St.

Delphos, OH 45833

419-695-4455

www.ktscelebrations.com

Your Wedding Cake

Your wedding cake is the focal point of the entire wedding menu. It is also a contender for the center of attention at your reception, as it sits in a place of honor for the guests to look at in awe. Many photographs of your wedding cake will be taken, from before the first slice to you and your groom feeding each other a bite.

The price of a wedding cake can begin quite low, if you make it yourself, and extend to thousands of dollars for premier bakers. You can expect to pay anywhere from $1.25 to $20 per slice, depending on numerous factors.

It Does Not Have to be White

Wedding cakes come in a variety of flavors and styles. If you do not want a white cake, you do not have to have one.

Although the flavors that you will ultimately choose from will vary depending on the baker, the following will give you an idea of what is available:

♥ Carrot   ♥ Lemon Chiffon   ♥ Almond

♥ Spice   ♥ Orange Chiffon   ♥ Hazelnut

♥ Chocolate   ♥ Raspberry Truffle   ♥ Red Velvet

♥ Mocha   ♥ Chocolate Mousse   ♥ Marble

Then, you will have to choose your filling. Some of the fillings available include the following:

♥ Hazelnut   ♥ Strawberry Mousse or Crème

♥ Raspberry   ♥ Chocolate Mousse or Crème

♥ Mocha   ♥ Amaretto Custard or Crème

♥ Pineapple   ♥ Lemon Mousse or Crème

♥ Cream Cheese   ♥ Many More

So, other than preferred taste, if you want something other than the standard white, these tips may help you choose:

♥ Spice and carrot are perfect flavors for autumn weddings, while rich flavors, such as red velvet and dark chocolate are perfect for winter weddings. If you are being married in the spring, consider lemon chiffon or another lighter flavor. Summer weddings are perfect for sponge cake with fresh fruit fillings.

♥ Consider the season. If your wedding is in the summer, some fillings and frostings may melt in the hot weather.

♥ Some fillings and flavors will cost more money than others. Always ask for a price list before making your choice.

♥ Consider using several different flavors for each layer of the cake. Thus, if some of your guests dislike chocolate, they will have another choice.

♥ One fun idea is to choose three different flavors. You pick your favorite, your fiancé picks his favorite, and then choose a third flavor — white may be a good choice — to be offered for mass appeal.

Wedding Cake Icings

Icing is part of what will make your cake beautiful. Not only should it taste good, but it should transform your cake into a work of art. Here is a little information to help you decide what you want.

♥ **Fondant icing** is smooth and neat and does not look like icing at all. Unfortunately, fondant is also expensive, does not taste all that great, and is extremely difficult to cut through. If you have your heart set on fondant, then by all means, go for it. Just realize it is not meant to taste good — it is meant to look good.

♥ **Butter Cream icing** is not too rich, has a great taste, and will allow almost any decorating you would like to be done. It is not as expensive as fondant, and the smooth look of fondant can be duplicated with butter cream icing.

♥ **Whipped Cream icing** is deliciously light and well-priced, but unfortunately, it does have some drawbacks. It does not hold up well in high heat or humidity, and it does not lend itself well to many types of decorations. However, if your wedding is not in the heat of summer, whipped cream icing is absolutely breathtaking when used in combination with fresh fruit or fresh flowers as decoration.

Wedding Cake Styles

Grab those wedding magazines again and start flipping through the pages. Look for styles of cakes that appeal to you. Your choices will be between layered, tiered, and different shapes — from round to oval to heart to square. After you have an idea of the look you like, clip out some examples and store them in your wedding cake file. You will need it when visiting area bakeries.

CASE STUDY: CRUMBS OF PARIS

What is your area of expertise?

Wedding cakes — I design, plan, and execute wedding cakes from the simplest to the more elaborate designs.

I also design the inside of the cake based on the taste and needs of the bride (sugar free, gluten free, etc.).

What are the most common mistakes you see that result in the bride and groom going over budget?

In many cases, the couple wants to make their wedding cake so unique that they design their own wedding cake. In most cases the results are not at all what they had expected, and they end up being disappointed.

It is very important that the couple trust their baker/designer. A good baker should be able to show the client his or her own work and not simply cut-outs from magazines. Also, if the couple is spending a considerably large amount of money on their cake it may be a good idea to purchase a six-inch decorated cake with the design of their choice; it shouldn't be that expensive, and it would give them the opportunity to see the quality of the cake and the skill in cake decorating.

If you could offer one piece of advice to a couple planning their own wedding under a budget, what would it be?

Go for the flavor. If the baker does not have lots of experience in cake decorating, purchase a completely smooth cake with borders only. The bride can always make a few nice flower arrangements with silk flowers and ribbons, or if the budget allows for fresh flowers, go for it. Fresh flowers or silk make any cake look beautiful, simple, and elegant, and best of all, they are very affordable. Also, just petals sprinkled on the cake can be a good idea. If the bride wants a more sophisticated look she can purchase sugar flowers from us or any other store online. That may add to the cost of the cake, but it may be worth it.

What are overlooked areas of savings?

In some cases, when the number of guests gets out of hand, it is a good idea to order a small wedding cake and then order just plain sheet cakes (no decoration, just borders). They usually get served in the kitchen previous to the cutting ceremony, so it makes serving the cake a breeze and is a big savings tip.

How do a bride and groom stay on budget?

Start with the cake of your dreams and go from there. If you cannot afford it, think of the same design but on a much smaller scale and add sheets for the rest of the servings. Cupcake wedding cakes can be elegant, fun, and an inexpensive option.

CASE STUDY: CRUMBS OF PARIS

A six-inch cake topper on top is unique and is also delicious. Also, using the same idea, but instead use a variety of nice mini pastries. This can be a very elegant solution for a low-budget wedding, and if you incorporate fresh flowers and ribbons, you have a winner. Don't have a nice cake stand? Go to your favorite hardware store and purchase clay pots and place them upside down, and add wooden circles in different diameters, then paint them in the color of your choice and add a ribbon to the edge of the wooden circles. .

What is the biggest misconception you see in wedding planning?

"Weddings have to be expensive to be impressive and elegant." Personally, I think simple elegance will never go out of style. Less is better and inexpensive.

How can a couple find quality services at the best price?

Do your homework first. Meet with bakers and taste and look at their work, ask what you can get for the least amount of money based on the number of guests you have, and go from there. First, you should love the flavor of the cake, and then you should feel that you can trust the baker with the execution of the decorating you desire. In some cases, if the budget allows, you can have your cake delivered from other cities. It can be expensive, but it may be worth it. Always remember, the last thing you eat at a party is dessert. Make sure the dessert is a good one. Or else don't waste your money on expensive food.

It's easy to become overwhelmed when planning a wedding. What is your advice for lowering the stress?

Let the professionals do their job. Just like in any other business, delegating can be the most difficult thing to do, but you have to trust those of us who are being paid to do the job. Make sure you have somebody in charge to call vendors a day or two prior to the event to make sure everything is okay. It avoids last-minute stress. Perfect weddings are not very common. It is the mistakes that make us remember a wedding. "Memorable weddings are not the perfect ones but the ones that weren't perfect."

Fernando Viveros

Crumbs of Paris

586 Broadway

El Cajon, CA 92021

619-440-4910

619-593-9245 (Fax)

www.crumbs-of-paris.com

Wedding Cake Tops

Tradition is the plastic bride and groom atop the wedding cake, but if you do not want to do this, you do not have to. Today, there are many different types of wedding cake tops available. Angels, doves, and cherubs are romantic choices that are beautiful for all types of weddings. You could also be humorous and put your favorite cartoon characters on top of your cake, such as Mickey and Minnie, Daisy and Donald, or even Popeye and Olive. If you collect other types of figurines, those would work as well. A couple of ideas for saving money are:

♥ Ask if the bakery you are purchasing your cake from offers a discount or a free cake top as an added benefit.

♥ Top your cake with a special item of yours, your fiancé's, or a family member's. This could be a crystal heart, a pair of antique figurines, or anything of appropriate size that has special meaning.

For some more ideas, check out Designs by Dorian, **www.designsbydorian. com**.

How Big of a Cake Do I Need?

The size and type of cake you choose will depend on how many guests you have. Keep in mind that a standard three-tiered cake will likely serve 50-100 guests. Five layers will serve 200 guests or more. Sizing will vary slightly, so be sure to ask your cake designer for exact numbers. A few ideas that may save you money are:

♥ If you plan on having a dessert table with other sweets offered, you can easily order a smaller cake and plan on smaller servings.

♥ Consider ordering a smaller tiered cake, decorated exactly as you want it, and then several sheet cakes to round out your serving size. Your end cost will be less, because sheet cakes cost approximately 75 percent less. That is a huge savings.

⌘Choosing the Bakerys⌘

Now that you know your likes and dislikes, it is time to choose your bakery. You have three sources to investigate when considering where your wedding cake will be created:

1. **Commercial Bakeries**, such as cake factories and grocery stores. Their prices will be reasonable, but their service will likely be less personalized. Commercial bakeries do not always offer as many choices in their wedding cakes, as part of the savings comes within their standard set of cakes. Smaller shops will likely have more personalized service with a few more options.

2. **Caterers and/or Reception Sites** may offer a wedding cake service. At times, you may find a great deal if you go this route. Other times, these types of services cost significantly more. The same goes with quality. Sometimes it is terrific; other times it is not.

3. **Small Bakers and/or Pastry Chefs** are where you will find the most creative, spectacular cakes. Although they can be difficult to find and are often of significant cost, the quality and appearance of your wedding cake will be superb.

When you begin searching for the bakery that will make your cake, here are a few ideas you may have overlooked, as well as some sources for recommendations:

❤ If your family has a regular bakery for birthday cakes, anniversaries, and other special moments, it may be your best bet. You already know it is reliable, you know if its cakes are a quality product, and even better — you may have a relationship with it already. This relationship may garner you a discount.

❤ If a friend was recently married and you admired her wedding cake, ask her who created it. Some bakers offer a discount based on referrals, so be sure to mention you were referred when contacting them.

♥ Other wedding industry professionals. Florists and photographers attend so many weddings that they may know who is the best in the business. Ask for their recommendations based on your needs.

♥ Ask the manager of your reception venue for a referral. He or she sees wedding after wedding and has certainly noticed what cakes stood out and which ones did not.

♥ Watch the advertisements in your newspaper for people who make wedding cakes from their home or as a side job. Be sure to ask for references and to see pictures if you go this route.

♥ Bridal shows are an excellent location to learn more about bakeries in your area. They also tend to have samples of their cakes to taste test.

Questions to Ask Your Wedding Cake Baker/Designer

As you begin looking around for the bakery to create your wedding cake, ask these questions:

♥ Will the cake designer create a custom cake, based on your specifications? If not, are there styles you can view to choose from? This is a good time to show any pictures you have clipped out.

♥ What are the most popular cake designs and flavors?

♥ Ask what types of ingredients the baker uses. Remember, the fresher the ingredients, the better-quality cake you will have.

♥ Can you sample any cakes? You will have an easier time deciding on flavors and fillings if you can taste test them.

♥ How many people are involved in the creation of your cake? Some bakeries use only one person per cake, while others have bakers and designers.

♥ When is the cake prepared in relation to your wedding? The less time the cake sits in the freezer, the higher quality it will be.

♥ If you decide to use fresh flowers to decorate the cake, does the baker work with your florist, or does it have another it does business with? This could affect your price, as you are more likely to receive a discount from the florist who is handling all your wedding day blooms.

♥ How many wedding cakes are being prepared for the same day as your wedding?

♥ Find out how the baker prices its cakes. Is it by the slice, which is the industry standard, or is it by the cake? Ask to see a price list that details the costs for flavors, fillings, and icings.

♥ Are there any extra charges you should be aware of?

♥ Many bakeries will throw in the top tier of the cake for free (this is the tier that couples save for their first anniversary). Ask if the bakeries you are considering offer this.

♥ Ask if the baker is licensed by the state health department. If it is not, you will want to look elsewhere.

♥ Does the bakery, or cake designer, deliver the finished wedding cake to the reception? If it does not, realize that you will have to arrange delivery, and wedding cakes in transit are an accident waiting to happen.

♥ Will the bakery pick up the cake board and pillars, if used, after the reception, or do you need to return them?

After You Choose

Believe it or not, wedding cakes get ordered incorrectly all the time. Even more common is the lost wedding cake that never makes it to the reception. Once you choose your bakery or independent cake designer, you will want to do the following:

♥ Receive a copy of your cake's order. Review this order carefully to ascertain if the baker has everything recorded correctly, specifically, the size, flavor(s), filling(s), icing, decorations, date of your wedding, location of your reception, and the correct phone numbers to reach you.

❤ Throughout the months prior to your wedding, call once or twice to confirm the delivery and your specific cake order. Ask any other questions you may have, and if anything alters in your order, get it in writing.

❤ Get a receipt for deposits and payments made.

Ways to Save — Your Wedding Cake

The following additional hints will help you stick to your cake budget:

❤ Do not order you wedding cake through a bridal salon. Although many bridal salons offer this service, it will cost you far more money.

❤ In most cases, you will get a lower price from a baker than a caterer.

❤ Comparison shop widely before making your final decision.

❤ Consider layers instead of tiers. Tiers cost more money.

❤ Avoid handmade sugar flowers and molded shapes to cut costs.

❤ When choosing your cake style, decorations, and the intricacies involved, realize that just like everything else — time is money. The longer it takes to make your cake, the more expensive it will be. Consider simpler decorations to save money.

❤ Fondant is expensive. You can get a similar look and better taste by using butter cream icing.

❤ Call a local craft store that offers cake decorating classes and ask if the teacher bakes and designs wedding cakes on a freelance basis.

♥ Do not overlook the "superstores." Wal-Mart, Sam's Club, and other superstores offer a tremendous deal on wedding cakes. They will let you sample them as well.

♥ Consider ordering wholesale. There are plenty of wholesale bakeries online. Check the online sources at the end of this chapter for a few.

♥ Make your own wedding cake or have someone close to you make it. You do not have to have a glamorous cake — just one that is attractive and tastes great. Check with **www.wilton.com** for ideas.

Online Sources — Wholesale Wedding Cake Suppliers, Supplies, and More

From pictures of wedding cakes to wholesale suppliers to wedding cake supplies, the following Web sites are chock-full of information:

♥ Bella Palermo Pastry Shop — **www.bellapalermo.com**

♥ Cakechannel.com — **www.cakechannel.com/wedding-cake-pictures.html**

♥ E Wedding Cake — **www.eweddingcake.com**

♥ Elegant Cheese Cakes — **www.elegantcheesecakes.com**

♥ Food Attitude — **www.weddingcakeonline.com**

♥ International Cake Exploration Societé — **www.ices.org**

♥ My San Diego Wedding — **www.mysandiegowedding.com/categories/cakes/index.html**

♥ Sugarcraft — **www.sugarcraft.com**

❧ The Groom's Cake ❧

The groom's cake has been a tradition in Southern culture for years and is beginning to show up at more and more wedding receptions. Traditionally, this cake was sliced and boxed specifically for the unmarried girls at the wedding. They were to take the slice home, place it under their pillow, and then they would dream about their future groom.

Today, the groom's cake is meant to be a reflection of the groom himself — his hobbies, likes, favorite sports, profession, alma mater, or anything else of significant value to him. Therefore, the groom's cake can be fun, but if you are trying to save money, it is easy to do so here. Here are some tips:

❤ Make the groom's cake yourself or, for more fun, have the best man and the groom's attendants make the cake. They will likely have a great time doing it, and some creativity may take place.

❤ Ask for a discount with your baker. Many bakeries offer the groom's cake at a reduced fee.

❤ Skip the groom's cake altogether if it is not important to your fiancé.

❧ Final Thoughts ❧

Your wedding cake should be the focal point of your reception, but that does not mean you have to spend much money on it. Be creative with your decorations, comparison shop widely, and be ready to make some hard money decisions. With a little forethought and creativity, you can truly have a luscious, tasty, and beautiful wedding cake — without spending a fortune.

Food and Beverages for Your Reception

Your reception is meant to be a party. This is the time to celebrate your marriage with your new husband, your family, and your friends. In addition to the fun aspect, it is also the first meal you will have as a married woman. You want the meal to be special. You want everyone to enjoy it. You also do not want to spend a ridiculous amount of money on it.

Unfortunately, the food and beverages you serve at your reception will take up the largest percentage of your wedding budget dollars. You can save money here, but to do so, prepare yourself for the time it will take to comparison shop, alter meal selections, and consider all the alternatives.

The Time of Your Reception

The first thing to consider is the time of day your reception is taking place. If you are having a morning ceremony, your reception food may be a simple brunch, in which case you will save considerably. Most receptions, however, are at the dinner hour, and this time of day has the highest food costs.

Morning or Noon Receptions

Morning or noon may be the most inexpensive reception time. You can easily serve a brunch with fresh fruit, salads, pastries, rolls, coffee, and juice. You will even save money with your wedding cake at this time, as you can plan on smaller servings. Depending on how large your wedding is, you may be able to enlist volunteers to purchase and lay out the food. Even if you do decide to hire a caterer, the cost will be significantly less than an evening meal.

Early Afternoon Receptions

After lunch and before dinner also offers some great possibilities in saving money. Depending on the exact time, you could serve a tea-type buffet with pastries, fresh fruit, some simple appetizers, and then, of course, your wedding cake. You may choose to offer champagne or wine, but your alcohol costs, overall, will be less than a later reception. Punches, sodas, coffee, and juices will round out the beverage cart nicely.

If you want to offer a little more fare than this, a small meal will work beautifully. Caesar salads with grilled chicken, pasta salads, a deli tray, and various fruits will fill the bill without breaking your budget.

Late-Afternoon Receptions

You have a few options with a reception taking place later in the day. If you are planning a short celebration, a meal is not a necessity. You could serve your wedding cake, punch, coffee, and maybe some champagne or wine.

If your reception will extend into the early evening, you will need to offer a meal to your guests. You could go light, however, with a sampling of hors d'oeuvres and a simple meal, such as grilled chicken and salad.

Early to Mid-Evening Reception

If your reception is in the early to mid-evening, you will likely want to serve a full meal. For this reason alone, an evening reception is the most expensive time of day to feed your guests. The fare you serve should be heartier than the light meal of a morning or afternoon reception. You will also want to include some hors d'oeuvres or appetizers before the main meal is served.

Late-Evening Reception

For a late-evening reception, you can choose to serve a full meal, or you can choose to do a dessert reception. You can offer a selection of desserts, along with your wedding cake, or you can skip the desserts in favor of the cake only. You can skip the alcohol altogether and simply supply coffee, tea, and other beverages.

Hire a Caterer or Do It Yourself?

Before you can make a decision on catering, you need to know what type of reception you are having, what type of food you want to serve, the level of formality, and how many guests you will be serving. Smaller weddings are easier to self-cater than larger ones. Casual gatherings are also easier to self-cater. More information on self-catering and hiring a caterer follow.

Self-Catering Your Reception

Many couples successfully self-cater their wedding reception and in the process are able to save a considerable amount of money. If you and your fiancé are considering going this route, there are a few things to think about.

You will need to estimate how much food you will need for your guests and spend considerable time comparison shopping to find the best deals. You will likely have to rent catering equipment such as warmers, serving trays, dishes, linens, and the like. You, family, or friends will need to prepare the food, and you will need volunteers or to hire additional help to set everything up at the reception so it is ready for your guests as they arrive. You will also need people to clean up after the reception. Self-catering is serious work, so be sure you have the commitment of family and friends to help. You will not be able to do it on your own, otherwise.

The following information will assist you if you will be catering the reception yourself:

❤ Talk to caterers and ask to see their menus. They do not need to know you are not considering hiring them. These menus will help you plan your appetizers and entrees.

❤ Use the season of your ceremony to plan out your menu. Choose foods that are in season and are universally inexpensive, such as chicken and pasta.

❤ Ask your friends and family for their favorite recipes, especially ones they have used to serve large groups of people.

❤ If you are considering a new recipe, do not wait until your reception to try it out. Have a taste test party for all the foods you are unsure of, and see which recipes go over well and which ones do not.

❤ Ascertain that if you need a kitchen to work with at your reception venue, that one is provided. If you need a refrigerator, for example, and it does not have one for you to use, you will have to consider other options.

❤ For more information on planning food for your reception, check out **www.angelfire.com/bc/hobbyhorse/index.html**.

Self-Catering Presentation

The presentation of your reception food can equal that of a professionally catered reception just by following a few tips of the trade:

❤ Garnish your food trays. For some great examples and how-to tips, check out this article: **http://homecooking.about.com/od/garnishing1/Garnishing_and_Food_Presentation.htm**

❤ Decorate the buffet and other food tables with flowers, bowls of fruit, wedding memorabilia, even framed pictures of you and your fiancé.

Ways to Save — Self-Catering

By planning ahead, you can save considerable money by cutting out the caterer. Here are a few other ways to save if you are self-catering:

♥ Plan on shopping in bulk. The more you buy of something, the less expensive each unit is, so check out warehouse stores, wholesale markets, and restaurant supply stores.

♥ When comparison shopping, be sure to look at the unit price to discover the real cost of what you are buying. Sometimes, a deal is not a deal.

♥ Find friends and family and borrow the supplies you need. If you have to rent every item, you may be better off going with a caterer.

♥ Purchase foods that are in season. If you want strawberries on your menu, but your ceremony is in December, you will pay extra for that.

♥ Visit your grocery store's deli counter and ask for a price list on their trays of food. Then, if you purchase appetizers from them, simply place them on your own serving trays, and you have a catered-quality look at an almost homemade cost. The best selection will come from grocery stores with a large deli area, with many different prepared selections to choose from.

Hiring a Caterer for Your Reception

Most couples decide to hire a caterer, and a good one can make all the difference between a "so-so" reception and an "absolutely fantastic" reception. Before beginning the search for your caterer, you should know the two types of caterers you will come across:

1. **In-house Caterers or On-premise Caterers** are those who provide the catering specifically for the venue of your reception. These caterers are found in hotels, country clubs, and other types of reception sites.

Many of these sites will not allow you to hire an off-premise caterer. Therefore, you should first ascertain if this is the case.

2. **Off-premise Caterers** bring the food into the reception location and set it up for you. They will fill the buffet table, appetizer table, the serving trays, and any other presentation needs that are required. In fact, these types of caterers are often full-service and will work with you to develop exactly what you need for your reception.

Locating an affordable caterer that delivers top-quality service can be quite a task. Most caterers do not advertise, as most of their work comes to them from word of mouth. When you are beginning to search for your caterer, consider these hints and tips to get you started:

❤ Ask the manager of your reception venue, provided it does not offer in-house catering, for referrals.

❤ Check the Yellow Pages.

❤ A friend or family member that was recently married can help. If you attended the reception and enjoyed the food and the presentation, ask them whom he or she used. Also, some caterers give discounts based on referrals, so make sure to ask.

❤ Visit wedding shows. Caterers will often have their menus, price listings, and other information on hand. Plus, you will get a chance to talk one on one with them.

When you have a list of possible caterers, the next step is deciding which caterer you will eventually hire.

❤ Compare their fees, naturally, but also ask about other necessities, such as if they provide linens, equipment, and dishware, and if so, what their prices are.

♥ When possible, use the telephone to ask the basic questions. You will likely cross several off your list at this stage, which means fewer personal visits to make time for.

♥ Always ask for references. You will get the best and most accurate information from past clients. Try for three to five references and call them. People are often more than happy to share their experience.

♥ Check to see if the caterer is a member of the International Food Service Executive Association. If not, it does not mean the business is not a great caterer, but those that are will have specific training; plus, all members will have met the requirements of the association. For more information on the IFSEA, visit: **www.ifsea.com**.

♥ Call the Better Business Bureau to see if any complaints have been made against the caterers you are considering. Negative marks should be taken seriously.

♥ Trust your instincts. If you get a bad vibe from someone, trust it and move on. Some things to watch for: Are staff members friendly and willing to answer your questions? Are they organized, in control, and seem knowledgeable? If you are not comfortable, move on.

Questions to Ask Caterers

When you have your list narrowed down to your top choices, it is time to get serious and make a visit to each of the caterers. You should plan on asking them the following questions:

♥ Do they specialize in a specific type of food and/or service? If so, what type?

♥ Ask to see photographs of prior receptions the caterer has handled.

♥ Ask for references from previous clients.

❤ Will they supply you with sample menus?

❤ Can you taste test the foods you are considering for your reception?

❤ Do they work with fresh foods? Frozen? Both?

❤ What is their average price range? Ask for a price list so you can see for yourself what everything costs.

❤ How involved in the reception are they? Do they work as a wedding coordinator and take control of each aspect of the reception, such as signaling when you should cut the cake? If so, is this an extra charge?

❤ If you hired them, who is your main contact? Make sure you have their business card, with phone number and e-mail information. Will they be available for questions?

❤ How many weddings, if any, does the caterer have planned for your wedding date?

❤ If necessary, is the caterer able to provide tables, chairs, linens, and dinnerware? Is there an additional fee? Ask to see any of these items to determine quality and if they will merge well with your wedding style. If they do not, can they arrange rentals for you?

❤ Do they set the tables, including putting out place cards and favors?

❤ Do they provide wait staff, if necessary? Even if they do not, ask them for referrals and the number you should consider hiring.

❤ Where do they prepare the food? What type of facilities will they need on hand at the reception venue?

❤ Do they have a license from the health department? This is extremely important, as it will show you they have met specific standards.

❤ Do they have liability insurance?

- ❤ Does the caterer provide alcohol? If so, do you have to use it, or can you provide the alcohol on your own? If you can provide but wish for the caterer to handle it, is there an additional fee?

Ways to Save — Your Catered Wedding Reception

When you and your fiancé have made a decision on your caterer, there are ways to save on the bottom line. Consider these hints:

- ❤ Try to pick a menu that features foods that are in season and therefore less costly.

- ❤ Be sure to see a price list of every type of entrée and appetizer offered. Do this even if you think you know what you want. You may find a cheaper option you did not know about.

- ❤ Forgo exotic dishes. Simpler foods cost less.

- ❤ Even expensive dishes have less expensive options to choose from. If you have your heart set on filet mignon, for example, medallions of beef will be just as tasty but with a smaller price tag.

- ❤ Consider combination plates that feature a small portion of the more expensive dish but a large portion of something less expensive, like chicken. It is a nice compromise.

- ❤ Select a unique meal that will cost less. Ask your caterer for suggestions.

- ❤ Avoid the most expensive options, such as lobster tail.

- ❤ If you wish to offer your guests more than one choice for an entrée, consider one non-meat dish. Pasta, for example, is an excellent choice and is budget friendly.

- ❤ Skip the dessert tray. You have a glorious wedding cake, which is all the dessert you need.

♥ Have your caterer prepare the food and deliver it but have volunteers set it up at the reception and clean it up afterward.

♥ You do not have to hire your caterer for the entire menu. Consider hiring a caterer to prepare and present the entrée only, while you (including family and friends) prepare appetizers.

♥ Negotiate. If you have a set budget in place, and you like one particular menu that is over your budget, ask the caterer what it can do that would be similar but less expensive.

♥ Consider the labor involved with your menu choices. Some appetizers, for example, that use only simple, low-cost ingredients, can be quite expensive because of the labor involved in the presentation. Choose simple ingredients and a simple presentation.

♥ Tell the caterer you do not want to see the wedding menus, but you do want to see other menus. Often, wedding menus are more expensive simply because they are titled "wedding."

♥ Although it may sound silly, skip having wait staff walk around with trays of appetizers. Setting up a table will cost less than the wait staff, plus, it will get people up and out of their chairs to mingle more.

♥ If there is a culinary school in your locality, see if it offers catering services. You could get an amazing presentation for the cost of the food only, or if there is a fee for labor, it will be quite small.

♥ Look for independent caterers who operate from their home. Their overhead will be smaller, which will be reflected in their fees.

Beverages for Your Reception

Serving alcohol at your wedding reception is an individual choice. Some couples are completely against it. There is no wrong choice here. If you do not want to serve alcohol, you certainly do not have to. There are a variety of nonalcoholic beverages that can be served, in addition to the standard soft drinks, juices, teas, and coffees. You can serve sparkling cider, sparkling grape juice, and mock alcoholic drinks to add a bit of flair.

For other couples, there is no choice — they will definitely serve alcohol. If you and your fiancé have not yet decided if you want to serve alcohol, or if you already know you want to but need to find a way to keep the costs down, read on.

The first thing to consider is your wedding budget. Offering alcohol adds to the cost of your wedding in a big way, so be sure you can afford it. That being said, there are ways to save money by being creative.

Cash Bar — Bad Etiquette or Not?

There is controversy surrounding the cash bar. In the past, having a cash bar as opposed to an open bar was considered bad etiquette for weddings, but that is not necessarily the case any longer.

For one, liability is an issue. When you place the decision to drink onto your guests' wallets, they may not drink as much as they would have otherwise. Also, your wedding reception should be about celebrating your marriage. Your guests are your family and friends, and they are there to celebrate with you, not for the "free booze."

Cash bars are a great way to offer alcohol to your guests without going over budget. Depending on how you go about it, you can use this option to great success, without being called cheap by your guests. Here are a few ideas.

♥ Set a cap amount that fits into your budget for alcohol. Offer an open bar until this amount has been met, and then switch to a cash bar. In this way, your guests will still be able to enjoy a few drinks on your tab, but you will be comfortable in knowing that you will not go over budget.

♥ Choose two types of wine, and maybe a small selection of beer, to serve at no cost to your guests. If they decide they want a different type of wine, beer, or a mixed drink, they pay for it themselves.

♥ Offer an open bar for the first two hours (or any amount of time you are comfortable with), and then switch to a cash bar.

♥ Or use a combination of the above choices, such as offering wines and beers for free for the first two hours, then opening the cash bar.

The choice is up to you. If you and your fiancé do not drink at all but you want your guests to be able to, that is another reason to go the route of the cash bar. You can even state this in your wedding invitations, on your reception card.

If, on the other hand, you and your fiancé are completely against having a cash bar but would like to offer alcohol to your guests, there are some basic facts you should know.

Who Provides the Alcohol?

You have a couple of different choices here. Many reception venues will offer you the choice of providing your own alcohol or using their bar. Some reception venues do not offer you this choice, and part of your contract will state that all alcohol is to be purchased by them. This is the first thing you need to determine.

Alcohol Provided by Your Reception Venue

Every reception location will have a different policy on serving alcohol. If your venue requires that it purchases your alcohol, you need to find out if:

1. It bases its fees on a flat fee, per-person rate

2. It bases its fees on the total consumption

3. Or it offers both and the choice is up to you

What you need to understand about the above is that, depending on your guests, one type of fee-based structure could cost far less than another. For example, if your guests are heavier drinkers, you will likely do better with the flat fee, per-person rate. However, if your guests, for the most part, are light drinkers, the consumption rate may be a smaller dollar amount.

When considering which fee structure to use, you want to ask what the flat fee is per person and if there is a discount for a large amount of guests. You also want to see the price list it will use for the consumption-based fees. Compare them, consider your guests, and choose.

Alcohol Provided by You and Your Fiancé

Providing the alcohol for your reception can save you money. This is because you can choose which types of alcohol to offer, and therefore, you can choose middle to inexpensive labels.

Ask your caterer, if you are hiring one, if it provides bar service. If it does, make sure it knows you are supplying the alcohol and you need only the actual bar service. This is important; otherwise, you may end up with a contract that stipulates it provides the alcohol, which is another middleman to pay.

If your caterer does not offer bar service or will not do it if you provide the alcohol, you will either need to hire a separate bar service, or to ask for volunteers to man the bar for you. Your reception venue may have staff that can handle the bar duties, so be sure to ask. If it does, you need to determine if the extra fee is affordable.

Depending on which way you eventually go, you may need to provide the glasses, the cocktail napkins, and drink stirrers. Many companies offer these along with their bar service, but some do not. Also, if you have volunteers perform the bar service for you, you will definitely need to provide these extra items. In addition, you will likely want special toasting glasses. Here are some ideas if you need to provide the supplies:

♥ Cocktail napkins and drink stirrers can be purchased in bulk at any party store at a reasonable price.

♥ Glasses can be purchased or rented. If you purchase, you will want to find plastic glassware, but look for high quality. You do not want to serve your guests drinks in flimsy plastic glasses.

♥ If you want real glassware and your reception venue or your caterer cannot provide them for you, renting may be an option. See the chapter on renting wedding equipment for more information.

♥ If your wedding is small and casual, you may be able to borrow glassware from friends and family. If you do this, find ways to differentiate who loaned what to you. Long-stemmed wine glasses from your aunt could have a small white ribbon tied along the stem. You could also label the bottom of the glasses with a small sticker.

♥ Toasting glasses can be simple glasses or engraved glasses. Save money by having only your and your fiancé's glasses engraved. Purchase, or rent, plain glasses for everyone else.

Online Sources for Napkins, Stirrers, Plastic Glasses, and Toasting Glasses

All these items can be ordered on the Internet with great success. Here are a few Web sites to check out:

♥ 4 Your Party.com — **www.4yourparty.com**

♥ Branders.com — **www.branders.com**

♥ Catering Supplies — **www.cateringsupplies.com**

♥ Creative Designs Online — **www.creativedesignsol.com/glasses**

♥ Custom Wedding — **www.customwedding.com/gc130.htm**

♥ For Your Party — **http://foryourparty.com**

♥ My Wedding Reception Ideas — **www.myweddingreceptionideas. com/wedding_toasting_glass.asp**

♥ Promopeddler.com — **www.promopeddler.com**

♥ Wedding DJ For You — **www.weddingdjforyou.com**

Other Ideas for Serving Alcohol at Your Reception

If bar service for your wedding reception is too expensive for your budget, you can still offer alcohol. Consider the following:

♥ Offering champagne for a toast and then offering only soft drinks and other nonalcoholic beverages.

♥ Having a self-serve station with wine and beer as the only alcoholic choices. Without mixed drinks, you do not need to have a bartender serve your guests.

♥ Putting ice buckets on each table, with a bottle or two of wine in each, and allowing your guests to serve themselves. Figure enough wine for two or three servings per seated guest at each table. This way, they can have a glass when they arrive, one with dinner, and one after dinner.

♥ Offering a "signature" drink at your reception and no other alcohol.

Ways to Save on Alcohol

Here are a few more ideas to help keep your budget in check:

♥ Have the bar staff open only bottles of wine that are needed. Bar staff often will open wine in preparation, but you may end up paying for a full bottle of wine in this way. If bar staff open several bottles, the cost can add up by the end of the night.

♥ If you have to use the reception venue's alcohol service, arrange ahead of time to serve the less expensive brands only. There is no need to have the higher-priced brands on hand.

♥ Buy your champagne the week between Christmas and New Year's. You will save a tremendous amount of money, as this is the one time of year that champagne prices drop.

♥ Purchase only enough champagne so each guest can have one glass for the toast.

♥ Bottled beer adds up fast. Consider using a keg instead, as you will save money. One keg equals seven cases of beer.

♥ On a similar note, purchase a magnum of wine. Magnums of wine are twice the size of a regular bottle and are less expensive.

⁖ Final Thoughts ⁖

The reception costs are the largest portion of your wedding budget, but with careful planning and research, you can save big on the food and the alcohol at your reception. You have many choices, so talk it over with your fiancé. Between the two of you, you will be able to sort through what is important to you and what is not and find the best ways to cut dollars off of your reception budget.

You want your reception to be a celebration of your wedding and of your marriage, and that is how it should be. But you do not have to spend a fortune for this to happen. Remember, the celebration is much more in the sharing of this event with your family and friends than it is in the food and drinks you serve. By keeping that thought in mind, you will find it easier to shave where you need to and still have the party you want to have.

Entertainment at Your Reception

When considering the entertainment at your wedding reception, you have several choices. Some will cost more than others, but again, there is no wrong choice. This is your wedding, and the entertainment you and your fiancé choose should match your styles, tastes, and vision for your wedding.

You can have a disc jockey, a band, or even volunteers taking turns with the CDs. The first thing to consider is the size of your budget for entertainment. You can easily spend close to $1,000 on entertainment, but you can also spend far less.

Disc Jockey or Band?

What will a disc jockey do for your reception? What will a band do? Are either of these choices that much better than having a friend switch out music throughout the evening? Well, yes and no. It all depends on what you want. The following points may help you and your fiancé make your decision:

❤ What type of music do you want? If your dream is to have live music, you will want to look into bands. If you want your favorite songs to be played, by the original artists, then you will want a disc jockey.

❤ How much space will you have available at the reception venue? A band will require more space. If a stage is available, this will save space. A disc jockey requires less space, so if your venue has space limitations, you may want to consider going the way of a disc jockey.

❤ Look at specific entertainment packages from disc jockeys and bands. Compare what each offers and the prices. Then it is simply a choice of what fits into your vision and your budget better.

❤ Think about the guests that will be at your reception. A younger crowd will likely be more entertained by a disc jockey, but an older crowd will likely enjoy the appeal of a band.

❤ If you and your fiancé are solidly in the middle, do not rule out either a band or a disc jockey until you have interviewed them and compared what each can offer you.

Hiring a Disc Jockey

When you hire a disc jockey, you will get one disc jockey, possibly an assistant or two, their sound system, and an extensive variety of music. You may also receive specialized lighting and possibly karaoke for later in the night. All disc jockeys are different. Some specialize in certain types of music, while others are happy to play what you want.

Also, not surprisingly, disc jockeys cost considerably less than a band does. The average price for a disc jockey ranges from $50-175 per hour, but where you live, the services the disc jockey offers, and the popularity of the disc jockey can alter this figure drastically.

Something else to consider: If you want more of an entertainer than simply a disc jockey to play tunes, you want a disc jockey entertainer. This is the person that takes control of the reception by creating a party-like atmosphere. A disc jockey entertainer will host sing-alongs, plan special dances, and even announce the toast, the cutting of the cake, and any other special additions.

The bottom line is a good disc jockey will make your reception a blast. A mediocre disc jockey will play the tunes you want played but will stay pretty much in the background. If you want to hire a disc jockey, decide which type of disc jockey you want. This way, you can ask them the appropriate questions during the interview process so you will know you are getting what you want.

How to Find and Choose Your Disc Jockey

The following ideas will help you find the perfect disc jockey:

♥ Ask for referrals from anyone and everyone you know that has recently been married. Friends, family, coworkers, and neighbors may have a name or several they can pass on.

♥ Your Yellow Pages. Look under "disc jockey."

♥ Advertisements in your city's newspaper and community newspapers

♥ Ask the other wedding professionals you have hired. Your caterer, cake decorator, and reception venue manager will likely know who is good and will be happy to pass on names.

♥ Wedding announcements in the paper often list the entertainer.

♥ Associations — one great one to call is the American Disc Jockey Association at 301-705-5150 or visit its Web site at **www.adja.org** for names in your locality.

Questions to Ask Prospective Disc Jockeys

When you have a list of disc jockeys you are interested in, be ready to ask them the following questions. This will help you save time and stress, as you will be able to narrow your selection of disc jockeys down with a few telephone calls.

- ❤ Do they specialize in a specific type of music? If so, find out what kind to be sure you are happy with the selection they will have. This could include swing, pop, rock, country, current hits, and oldies.

- ❤ Are they willing to play a variety of tunes? A little country, a little rock, or whatever you and your fiancé's want?

- ❤ If you have certain songs you want played, but the disc jockey does not have them, will he or she pick them up? Or, as an alternate, will the disc jockey play your CDs?

- ❤ Can you or your guests request songs during the reception? And, if the disc jockey has those songs, will he or she be willing to play them?

- ❤ Will the disc jockey be on his or her own, or is there an assistant or assistants that come and help? If there are, can you also meet them?

- ❤ Does the disc jockey have his or her own equipment, or do you, or the reception venue, need to supply it?

- ❤ How much room will the disc jockey need for equipment? Will a table be needed?

- ❤ When is setup? It is preferable if he or she is ready to go when the reception starts.

- ❤ What will he or she wear? If your wedding is formal and the disc jockey shows up in jeans and a T-shirt, this is something you will want to know ahead of time. If you have a preference, as in a tuxedo or suit for a man, ask if he will comply.

♥ What is the minimum amount of time the disc jockey will play?

♥ Will he or she take breaks? How many and how often?

♥ Ask about prices for the average length of a reception, four hours or so, and, if there is a range, ask what encompasses the difference in price.

♥ Is he or she willing to stay over if the reception runs longer than expected? If so, is there a charge for the extra time, and how much?

Ways to Save — Your Disc Jockey

Here are a few ways to save money if you decide to hire a disc jockey:

♥ If you and your fiancé are interested in having ethnic music played and your disc jockey does not have what you want, there is no need to purchase it. Check out your local library and rent it instead.

♥ Specify the amount of breaks, and how long they can be, that your disc jockey can take. You may be surprised, otherwise, at the amount of breaks taken for the amount of money you are paying.

♥ Ask your friends and family to see if anyone has experience working as a disc jockey. You may be able to snag a volunteer to do the job for you for free.

♥ If you go ahead with a volunteer disc jockey, you and your fiancé can spend some time to make your own mixes for him/her to play. Not only will you and your fiancé have fun doing this, but you will be able to set the mood for your reception perfectly.

♥ Again, if you are using a volunteer, save your money. There is no need to buy a large amount of CDs, which on their own could end up quite pricey. Instead, borrow from family, friends, and the library.

♥ If you do not have a sound system, ask the reception venue if it can arrange one for you.

Hiring a Band for Your Reception

If you have your heart set on live music, you may want to consider hiring a band. Your other choices for live music are single musicians that play the violin, the guitar, or another instrument.

When you hire a band, there is much to consider, besides the price. A band can simply play music, but what you are likely looking for is a band that will play great music and entertain your guests. You want a band that will complement your vision for your wedding.

If your wedding is formal, with soft lights, champagne, and a gourmet meal, you may want a more sedate band. On the other hand, if you want a party atmosphere at your reception, you will want a lively band that will get people out of their seats and dancing.

The band's style is also important. After all, unless you and your fiancé love polka, you are not going to want a band that specializes in polka music. Bands come in all shapes and sizes, from a duo to a much larger orchestra, and the types of music they play will differ. If you are searching for an ethnic selection of music, the band you want will be different than a couple who wants the top 40 to be played.

How to Find and Choose a Band

How do you find the perfect band for your reception? It is as simple as talking to people and checking a few different resources. The following ideas will help get you started:

♥ Ask for referrals from anyone and everyone you know that has recently been married. Friends, family, coworkers, and neighbors may have experience with bands that they can pass on to you.

♥ Your Yellow Pages. Look under "orchestras and bands."

♥ Advertisements in your city's newspaper and community newspapers.

♥ Ask the other wedding professionals you have hired. Your caterer, cake decorator, and reception venue manager will likely know the hot and happening bands in your area.

♥ Wedding announcements in the paper often list the entertainer.

♥ Music schools at local colleges and universities. Just call and ask for recommendations, as many music students have bands and will play for a great price.

♥ Your local symphony organization, for leads on symphony musicians that may play at social functions.

Questions to Ask Prospective Bands

When you have a list of bands you are interested in, be ready to ask them the following questions. This will save you time in narrowing your selection.

♥ Do they have a signature sound or a specific type of music they specialize in? You want to know if they are into classics, rock, pop, country, or jazz, to name a few.

♥ Are they willing to play a variety of styles? This is especially important if you and your fiancé have drastically different tastes in music.

♥ If you have certain songs you want played, and the band is not familiar with them, are they able and willing to learn it for your reception? Do you need to supply the sheet music?

♥ Can you or your guests request songs during the reception? If they know the music, will they be willing to play these songs?

♥ How many members make up the band? Ask for their names, and ask if you can listen to them play. Also, find out if there are alternates that take the place of a member if one becomes ill.

♥ Will the band members bring their own equipment, or do you need to supply it? If you need to supply it, what do they need? Find out if your reception venue has these items.

♥ Do they prefer a stage, or are they all right without a stage as long as there is ample space? How much space do they need?

♥ When do they come to set up? It is preferable that they be ready to go when the reception starts.

♥ Do they dress casually or in suits? In tuxedos? If you have a preference to style of dress, will they comply?

♥ What is the minimum amount of time the band will play?

♥ Will they take breaks? How many and how often?

♥ Ask about their prices for the average length of a reception, four hours or so, and, if there is a range, ask what encompasses the difference in price.

♥ Are they willing to stay over if the reception runs longer than expected? If so, do they charge for the extra time, and how much?

Ways to Save — Your Band

If you decide to hire a band, here are a few examples of ways you can cut costs, as well as other ideas to be sure you do not pay more than you should:

♥ Always listen to the band before hiring them. It is even better if you can sit in for a few songs at a reception they are playing. Although you may be tempted to pay extra money for a hot band, if you do not hear them first, you may find they are not right for your wedding. That is money wasted.

❤ If you are paying for five hours of play time but they play for only three because of large amounts of breaks, you are losing money. Be sure break information is included in your contract. That way, if they exceed the listed break time, you can ask for a discount.

❤ Check with area music schools. There may be awesome bands made up of students that will charge you a significantly lower rate.

❤ Cut the band's playing time in half by having them start later or leave earlier. Fill in the blank time with a volunteer disc jockey from your group of friends or family.

❤ Look for a smaller band size. The more members means the higher the cost, as it will be split among the members.

❧ Valuable Entertainment Info ❧

In addition to the above information, these hints will help you with any type of entertainment you hire for your wedding reception.

❤ Give the disc jockey and/or band a list of songs you and your fiancé would like to hear at the reception. This will help ensure that those songs are played, but it will also clue your entertainer into what type of music should be the focus.

❤ Ask the reception venue if it can pipe music into the reception during the entertainer's breaks. If so, there will not be any "dead" air time, and you will not have to find a way to fill in the gaps.

❤ Compare all prices. You want to know price per hour and flat rate fees in combination with the total hours your reception will span. This is the only way to determine who is charging you the least amount of money for the services.

❤ Extra fees can add up. Always be aware of any additional fees that may pop up.

❤ Always get it in writing. Whatever was discussed and agreed on should be put into a contract with signatures. This means if you are hiring a four-person band, all four people should sign the contract.

❤ Make sure you have a receipt for any payments you make, including deposits and final payment. Keep that, along with a copy of your check, in your entertainment file.

Online Sources — Entertainment

Here are some online sources to give you more information on entertainment for your wedding. Some are fun, and some are informative:

❤ Here is a listing of the top 200 songs played at wedding receptions: **www.discjockeys.com/top_200.php**.

❤ For some ideas on wedding receptions, including theme, style, and entertainment, check out this article: **www.pinkfridge.com/lal_weddings/reception-ideas.htm**.

❤ Customized songs made personally for you and your fiancé: **www.songsmadeforyou.com**.

❤ More information on selecting the right disc jockey for your wedding can be found here: **www.weddingapproved.com/help/wedding_dj.html**.

❤ This is a site on entertainment at weddings. Have fun going through its ideas. **www.enhancentertainment.com.au/weddings3.asp**.

❤ Some more ideas for entertaining your guests that go beyond music: **www.thefrontdoor.com/Ideas_Wedding_Reception_Entertain_Guests.cfm**.

♥ A list of the most popular first dances can be found here: **www.1877yourmusic.com/weddingreceptionclassics.html**.

✥ Final Thoughts ✥

Your wedding reception should be a dynamic celebration of your marriage. When planning the entertainment, do not forget to keep the likes and dislikes of you and your fiancé in the forefront. This is your day. Although you do want your guests to have a good time, it is far more important that everything that happens on this day is a reflection of you, your fiancé, your love for each other, and the commitment you are making.

Entertainment is one of those areas where it is far too easy to go overboard. When interviewing entertainers and deciding on the best entertainer for your reception, remember you made your wedding budget for a purpose. Try hard not to be swayed by the excitement of the moment. If a band or disc jockey is over your budget and there is no way to lower the cost, you should refocus and move on to the next person on your list.

If you take the time to research, interview, and focus on sticking to your budget, you will be able to find the right entertainment for your wedding reception. Then, after your ceremony, you will be able to relax and celebrate.

Renting Equipment

Depending on the resources you choose to take advantage of, where your ceremony and reception are held, and your specific needs, you may find yourself needing to rent equipment for your wedding ceremony and reception. This could encompass everything from glassware, dishes, tables, chairs, and linens to a dance floor and a tent.

This chapter will give you some of the ins and outs of renting what you need, and the best prices you can find.

Renting Versus Buying

Many couples make the mistake of purchasing much of the equipment they will need for their wedding, and their budget takes a serious hit because of it. Almost anything you may require for your ceremony and reception can be rented, and that will save you a large amount of money over outright purchasing.

What Are You Renting?

Almost any necessity you have can be rented. There are far too many rentable items to list here, but this chapter does hit the main items many couples need to rent. Here are a few to keep in mind and some pointers to help you along the way.

Rent a Tent

If you are having your wedding ceremony or reception outside, you will want to rent a tent to protect your guests from possible bad weather and to shade them from the sun.

The first important consideration is placement of the tent. The best location for a tent is on high, level ground. After you have found the best spot, check it after it rains to see if there are any large pooling spots of water. If there are, you may want to find another location.

The next consideration is the size of the tent. The size of your tent should comfortably fit the amount of guests you plan to have, and it should be able to easily encompass tables and chairs, set up. Another consideration to keep in mind is the purpose of the tent. You will want more room if dinner is going to be served than you will if you are serving only drinks and dessert.

An easy formula to follow for a dinner tent is to allow at least 12 square feet per person if you are using round tables, and at least ten square feet per person if you are using rectanglular tables. If you are serving cocktails only, you can plan for less room. Figure, instead, six square feet per person. This formula will also work well for a ceremony tent.

Types of Tents

There are several styles of tents available to rent, and each offers something different in appearance and in sheltering ability. These styles are:

Clear Span Frame Tents

This type of tent does not use a middle tent pole but instead are freestanding vinyl and pipe structures. Clear span frame tents are more expensive than standard tents, costing about 40 percent more. However, they fit better into tight spaces and have more internal room for your guests. In addition, they are the easiest type of tent to keep cool or to heat up, depending on the season. Another great feature is that they are sturdy, which means you can hang objects from the ceiling, such as a sound system or speakers.

Pole Tents

Pole tents are the traditional tent and the type most often rented for celebrations. They are less expensive than clear span tents and are ideal on grass or sand because of the staking system used. Of course, these tents also have center poles that are a hindrance to sight and mobility. If you are on a tight budget, however, and need to rent a tent, a pole tent will suit your needs and your budget.

Tent Accessories

Rental firms will have all the accessories you may want for your tent, such as flags, lanterns, columns to conceal the poles, canopies, valances, and even wall and ceiling liners meant to disguise the mechanics of the tent. You can seriously dress up your tent so it has the appearance you want for your wedding ceremony and/or reception. Just be careful, as each accessory will add to the final price tag.

What to Know

Tents come in a variety of colors, from stripes to solids. They can even be translucent. However, some shades will cost more than others. Also, your tent will need to be set up at least one full day before your wedding, preferably two to three days ahead of time. This will allow you and your wedding professionals to get your tables and chairs set up, to decorate, and anything else that needs doing, in plenty of time for your big day.

The cost of renting your tent will be determined by the size, style, accessories, and setup charges. Also, if the site needs extensive prep work before the tent can be placed, this will add to your charges. Other additional charges that may apply are:

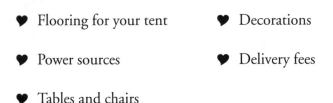

❤ Flooring for your tent   ❤ Decorations

❤ Power sources   ❤ Delivery fees

❤ Tables and chairs

Saving money on renting a tent is not an easy task. You will want to comparison shop widely. When you do, you want to be sure to compare equally. Look at delivery charges, accessories, setup, takedown, and anything else you are interested in having the rental company take care of for you. Ascertain that there are no hidden charges.

In addition, there are some steps you can take to save some money:

❤ Decorate the tent yourself with your own supplies. You will pay a premium if you rent them along with your tent.

❤ If you are renting several things from the same company, ask about a bulk discount.

❤ Ask about package deals. If you are also renting a dance floor, tables and chairs, and anything else, the business may have a "party package" price that will save you some money.

❤ If the tent is going to be set up at the beach or another public location, rather than your backyard, find out if any other weddings are happening within 24 hours. You may be able to work out a deal with the other wedding couple to split the costs.

♥ Decorate the tent with inexpensive flickering Christmas lights for a beautiful glow. If you go this route, try to pick up the lights immediately after Christmas, when they will be the least expensive.

♥ Borrow potted plants from friends and family and use those to decorate the inside and the outside of the tent.

♥ Watch for deals. Often, just before peak wedding season, rental companies offer bargains on their services. Try to book them then, even if your wedding is not until later in the year.

Rent a Dance Floor

You likely will not have to rent a dance floor if you are having your reception at a hotel, club, or other reception venue. If you are having your reception somewhere else, where a dance floor is not provided, you will need to decide if you want to rent one.

You can rent a dance floor through many of the party rental stores. You can also check with your caterer to see if it has any recommendations.

What to Know

Wood parquet flooring is no longer the only choice in renting dance floors. There is a great deal of variety and flexibility in dance floor choices. Some things to consider are:

♥ Plastic-based dance floors are able to withstand many different climates and moisture levels.

♥ With the plastic-based dance floors, you will find a nice variety in colors and designs.

♥ Setup is easy and can be done by just a few people.

♥ Black-and-white dance floors make for a dramatic focus.

♥ Slate-hued dance floors are the newest trend.

♥ If you and your fiancé enjoy the wood look, it is still a fashionable choice. Wood and wood-like parquet floors remain the traditional favorite.

Saving money on renting a dance floor is about comparison shopping. Caterers and party rental stores are the most common places to rent a dance floor, so a few hints are:

♥ Ask about discounts if you are renting other items from the same company.

♥ Watch for seasonal specials that are sometimes offered.

♥ You may not need a huge dance floor. Consider how many guests you have coming. Out of those, a percentage will likely never dance. You may not need as large a floor as you think.

♥ Do not hesitate to ask if there is any way to receive a discount when placing your order. You may find out that a dance floor you had decided against, because it was more expensive, can be rented at a lower price.

Renting Tables and Chairs

If your reception venue does not provide tables and chairs, you will first want to ask your caterer if it does. You will have to provide the tables and chairs for your guests if it does not or if you are not hiring a caterer and your wedding ceremony and/or reception is not being held in a traditional location. Your needs, the amount of your guests, and the type of reception you are having will dictate how many tables and chairs you will need.

For your ceremony, you will want to be sure you have enough seating for all the guests. No one should be left standing.

For your reception, it will depend on the type of reception you are having.

If you and your fiancé are serving a full meal, you will want enough tables and chairs for all your guests. However, if you are simply having a cocktail reception, you need only to provide tables and chairs for approximately 50 percent of your guests, as people will arrive at different times and not everyone will sit at the same time.

What to Know

When it is time for you to rent your tables and chairs, there are various styles for you to consider. The traditional, and most common, style of chair for wedding receptions is white wooden or plastic chairs. The traditional, and most common, style of tables chosen for wedding reception is round tables that seat eight guests per table. If you would like more guests per table than the standard eight, consider renting rectangular tables.

Even if you go with round tables, when you are planning the bridal party table, you will likely want a rectangular table or even a set of rectangular tables placed end to end, depending on the size of your wedding party.

Again, as in all rental equipment, the price you get is somewhat hard to negotiate. What you should do when contacting rental companies for tables and chairs is:

♥ Comparison shop widely.

♥ When contacting rental companies, ask them about the types of tables and chairs they offer. Make sure they know the size of your wedding; the formality of your wedding; and if the locality is outside, inside, or within a tent.

♥ Do not forget to ask for a price list, and be sure there are no hidden costs, such as for delivery and setup.

Renting Tableware and Linens for Your Wedding Reception

As with the tables and chairs, if your reception venue or your caterer does not provide tableware and linens for your wedding reception, you will need to provide them. If your wedding is casual, you can skip the step of renting and choose other options for your reception food, such as plastic tableware. However, except for the most casual of receptions, you will likely want traditional tableware.

What to Know

Here are a few pointers to help you get started:

- ♥ If your reception is a formal affair, with waiters and waitresses, the tablecloths you use are important. You can use white linens, or you can use a coordinating color that matches your wedding. However, you do want individual place settings for each guest.

- ♥ If your reception is less formal and encompasses a buffet, you will still want tablecloths. However, you can skip the individual place settings and have the tableware stacked at the buffet table next to the food.

- ♥ The type of linens and tableware you choose will highly depend on the formality of your wedding. You will want to discuss options with your caterer or, if you do not have one, with your rental company to select what will fit into your budget and into your wedding style.

When you are trying to fit tableware and linens into your budget and you find yourself faced with the necessity of renting the equipment, the following hints will help you find the best deals:

- ♥ After you know what type of tableware and linens you want, you will need to comparison shop.

- ♥ Ask about discounts if you are renting other equipment from the same rental company.

- ♥ Find out if there are bulk discounts. This is different than the previously mentioned hint. If you are having a large wedding, you should be able to negotiate a lower price since you are renting more tableware than an average-sized wedding.

Renting Glassware for Your Wedding Reception

Glassware is one of those items that will largely depend on the formality of your wedding. Glassware for your reception table can encompass everything from iced water tumblers and wine glasses to fluted champagne glasses and toasting glasses. It depends what you want at each place setting when the reception begins.

If you are having bar service, you may want a toasting glass, a water tumbler, and a coffee cup at each setting on your table. These items can also be rented from a rental supply company. Each point that was mentioned for tableware and linens stands true for glassware. Know what you want, comparison shop, and ask about discounts.

Where to Find Your Rental Supplier

The following tips will help you find a reputable rental supplier:

♥ Ask for referrals from family and friends. Rental companies are used for all types of gatherings, so you do not have to stick with people who have recently been married. Anniversary parties, birthday parties, and family reunions are all places that rental companies may have been used, so ask everyone you know.

♥ If you, your fiancé, or a friend or family member works for a company that uses a rental facility throughout the year for company functions, find out who that company is.

♥ The Yellow Pages. Look under "party supply," "rentals," or the individual item you are looking for, such as "dance floor."

♥ Advertisements in bridal magazines, local newspapers, and even commercials on television.

❤ Bridal shows are a terrific place to find many of the wedding industry professionals in your area, and rental facilities are no different.

Questions to Ask the Rental Company

When you begin to narrow your list of rental companies down, these questions will help you find the right one:

❤ Who is your contact person? Get their cell phone number and their e-mail address.

❤ How many years has the company been in business?

❤ What are its hours of operation?

❤ What are its days of operation?

❤ Does it have liability insurance?

❤ Can you see a full price list of all the items you require, along with delivery, setup, and any other fees that may be attached to the final bill?

❤ When will the items be delivered? How far in advance?

❤ When will the items be picked up after the event? The same day, the next day? Remember, if they cannot be picked up until the next day, you need to ascertain if you will have additional charges from the ceremony and/or reception venue.

❤ What is their payment policy? Do you have to pay a deposit? If so, how much? Be sure to get a receipt for every payment made.

❤ What is their cancellation policy? Get this in writing.

Ways to Save — Your Rental Company

Saving money is part and parcel with renting rather than purchasing the items you may need for your wedding ceremony and reception. Unfortunately, depending on how much you have to rent, it can still add up to a total that may exceed your budget. In addition to the points already mentioned, consider the following:

❤ Make a list of everything you think you will need to rent. Go through it with your fiancé, your wedding party, and even your family. Ask for advice on what is truly necessary and what is not. For example, renting potted plants may not be a necessity. You may be able to borrow them from friends and family and then simply cross them off your rental list.

❤ There may be items that you would like to have but are not considered necessary. Take these items and make a secondary list. If you have money left over in your wedding budget, you can pick and choose from this list.

❤ If you are using a rental facility that was referred to you by your employer, you may even be able to wrangle a discount using the company name — just confirm this before you do it.

Final Thoughts

Renting items for your wedding ceremony and reception is a good choice for the items you cannot afford to purchase or for those you cannot borrow. Just be sure to take your time in selecting what you need and to stay within your budget. With these two things in mind, you will not go wrong in renting those extras that will help make your wedding shine.

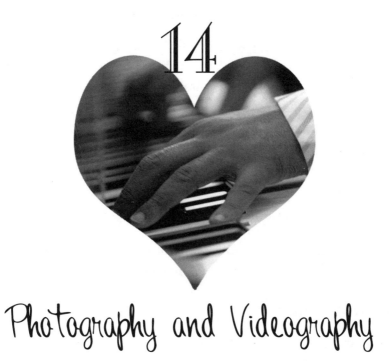

Photography and Videography

You have dreamed about your wedding day for a lifetime. You have planned it for months or even for years. When it arrives, you will be surprised at how quickly the day flies past. In addition to your memories of this day, you will want visual reminders that will bring back the emotions, the beauty, and the love of your wedding day. Photographs and video will do this for you.

Photographs for Your Wedding Day

The right photos will capture all the magic energy of your wedding day. The right photographer will deliver all the special moments, from the candid to the planned, that you can keep for a lifetime.

Photographs of your wedding day are, perhaps, one of the most important aspects for you to consider. You will proudly display these photos for the rest of your life. Your children and your grandchildren will someday view them. It is crucial to not underestimate the importance of the photographer at your wedding.

Of course, this can come with a hefty price tag. Average photography package costs for a wedding are in the $3,000 range. You can save money, though, and end up with the right photographer and the right photos, for a price that will fit in your budget. If you are tempted to splurge on any area of your wedding and you have saved money in other areas, your wedding photographs will last your entire life and may be a good place to invest those extra dollars.

Wedding Photographs — What Are You Purchasing?

When you make the choice to hire a professional photographer for your wedding day, what, exactly, are you purchasing, besides their expertise?

Candid Wedding Photos

Candid photographs are the ones you will likely cherish the most. These photos will catch the glimpse of pride and love in your parents as they gaze at you. These photos will grab the moment of enchantment when your father takes your hand for a dance. Candid photographs are the ones that will bring a tear to your eye and a smile to your face whenever you look at them. They will show the excitement, the love, the nervous energy, and all the emotions in between that occur on your wedding day.

Wedding Day Portraits

Portrait shots on your wedding day are the formal photographs that will be taken. These are the staged photographs with your family, your wedding party, or you and your new husband cutting into the wedding cake. Portraits are also photographs that are taken before the wedding day. Sometimes, these are taken in the photographer's studio. Other times, they are taken on location at the church, a park, or another venue. Often, the portraits taken before the wedding are used in the newspaper engagement announcement, on the wedding programs, and/or on the bride and groom's wedding Web site.

Wedding Day Albums

You will have a selection of albums to choose from to display your candid and portrait photographs. Some of these albums are quite pricey, and others are much more reasonable. Many photographers also offer a digital album, which is when the photos are printed on the album page instead of individual prints being put into the album page. Digital albums are also less pricey.

A few examples of wedding day albums can be found at the following Web sites:

♥ Art Leather — **www.artleather.com**

♥ Capri — **www.caprialbum.com**

♥ Image Designer — **www.image-designer.com/template/digitalalbum.htm**

♥ Leather Craftsmen — **www.leathercraftsmen.com**

CASE STUDY: BETHANY GILBERT PHOTOGRAPHY

What is your area of expertise?

I am a professional photographer specializing in fashion-style wedding photography. I work in a "photojournalistic" style focusing on the actual events and emotions of the day. I direct very little, other than formal portraits and pride myself on my ability to capture otherwise unnoticed situations.

What are the most common mistakes that result in the bride and groom going over budget?

Many brides choose their photographer based on price alone. Although budget restrictions are important and should be considered, the bride and groom will be much happier in the long run if they choose their photographer based on their skill, experience, and personality. It is very important that the bride and groom feel comfortable with their photographer.

If you could offer one piece of advice to a couple planning their own wedding under a budget, what would it be?

Choose a reputable photographer based on personal recommendation and experience. Ask married friends and relatives about their wedding photographer

CASE STUDY: BETHANY GILBERT PHOTOGRAPHY

and choose someone who comes highly recommended from someone you trust. Many brides waste money by choosing "cheaper" photographers who can't produce the same quality as experienced professionals. This may save money initially, but you will always regret not having your memories captured by a true professional.

What are overlooked areas of savings?

Many photographers will provide the couple with a CD of either the original files or the completed files. The original files are what you see right out of the camera. The completed files have usually been color-corrected, cropped, and further tweaked for final printing. The completed files are preferred. This saves money on prints and other items and allows more money to be budgeted for other things. Another option is to hire a less-expensive photographer for engagement or bridal portraits so that you can budget more toward photography for the wedding day.

How do a bride and groom stay on budget?

The couple should focus on what is important to them as far as time constraints, products, and prints. Some couples may not want a wedding album or large prints but would prefer a CD of the images and a couple smaller prints. Choose a package based on your individual needs or discuss "à la carte" options with your photographer. Some photographers will customize a package based on the individual items or images you would like.

What is the biggest misconception you see in wedding planning?

Couples tend to overspend on things that no one notices or things that are trends at the time. I think that they should spend more of their budget on larger things that are important to them as a couple. For instance, a bride may consider using music from their MP3 player for the dances instead of hiring a DJ. This would allow her to allocate more of her budget to things that are more important to her, such as photography.

What shouldn't the bride and groom do to cut costs?

The bride and groom shouldn't cut costs by hiring amateur photographers or students. This is a common suggestion but can cost the bride and groom in the long run when their photos fade or their albums or other products start to fall apart. It is better to budget wisely and in accordance to what is important to them as individuals.

Do you have an example to sharethat shows how a bride and groom saved money?

CASE STUDY: BETHANY GILBERT PHOTOGRAPHY

A recent couple asked that I create a custom package for them to fit their budget. They were willing to forgo some products and choose a less expensive coffee-table album instead of the usual leather-covered, flush-mount album in order to have me as their photographer. I created a package for them consisting of unlimited time (which is included in all of my packages) and a simple album which fit into their budget. Their pictures and album turned out beautifully, and they seem to be very happy with the results.

It's easy to become overwhelmed when planning a wedding. What is your advice for lowering the stress?

Try to focus on the meaning of the day rather than the decorations or the schedule. Hire a photographer and other vendors you trust so that you can enjoy your day without worrying about the photos, the cake, or the flowers. If something goes wrong, don't worry about it; most people won't notice anyway. They are focused on the beautiful bride.

How would a couple know when a price is truly "too good to be true"?

If a couple focuses on quality, relationships, and trust when choosing their wedding photographer and other vendors, the price is never "too good to be true." If they know that this vendor has their best interests in mind, then they can know that they will be treated fairly. Budget wisely, but do not choose vendors based on price alone.

Any other suggestions or advice you would like to share?

Relax! Focus on what is important — you are marrying the person of your dreams, and you should be looking forward to the happy life you have ahead of you. Hire professional, competent vendors and services, and leave the worrying to them.

Bethany Gilbert

Bethany Gilbert Photography

355 Trace Rd.

Laurel, MS 39443

www.bethanygilbert.com

BETHANY GILBERT
photography

Wedding Photographs — What Do You Want?

There are so many possible photos and shots you may want for your wedding. If you are not sure what to ask for, here is a selection of shots you and your fiancé may want to consider:

Photographs Taken before the Ceremony

Many couples decide to have formal portraits taken before the wedding day. These can either be taken in the studio or on location, such as in a park, on the waterfront, or another place that is special. If you and your fiancé have thought about this, the following poses are some of the most popular.

Photographs of the Bride

- ♥ A solo portrait of the bride in her wedding gown

- ♥ A portrait of the bride with her mother

- ♥ A portrait of the bride with her father

- ♥ A portrait of the bride with her mother and her father

- ♥ A portrait of the bride with her siblings

- ♥ A portrait of the bride with her maid of honor

- ♥ A portrait of the bride with her entire bridal party

- ♥ A portrait of the bride with another special friend or family member. This could be your best friend from high school or college, your grandmother, your grandparents, or any other relationship you have that is special to you.

Photographs of the Groom

- ♥ A portrait of the groom in his tuxedo

- ♥ A portrait of the groom and his father

- ♥ A portrait of the groom and his mother

- ♥ A portrait of the groom with his father and his mother

- ♥ A portrait of the groom with his siblings

- ♥ A portrait of the groom with his best man

- ♥ A portrait of the groom with his best man and his groomsmen

- ♥ A portrait of the groom with another special friend or family member. This could be a best friend from high school or college, his grandfather, his grandparents, or any other relationship that is special to him.

Photographs Taken at the Wedding Ceremony

- ♥ Your guests arriving at the church or ceremony venue

- ♥ The ushers escorting your guests to their seats

- ♥ The guest book attendant

- ♥ The bride and her father arriving at the ceremony and getting out of the car

- ♥ The grandparents being seated

- ♥ The groom's parents being seated

- ♥ The mother of the bride being seated

- ♥ The groom and the groomsmen standing at the altar

- ❤ Your attendants' processional down the aisle

- ❤ The ring bearer and flower girl

- ❤ The bride and father processional

- ❤ The bride and groom exchanging their vows

- ❤ The exchanging of rings

- ❤ When the bride and groom kiss

- ❤ The lighting of the Unity Candle

- ❤ The bride and groom walking up the aisle

Photos After the Ceremony but Before the Reception

Often, formal pictures are taken immediately after the ceremony before arriving at the reception. You can have these taken at the ceremony venue, or you can choose another location, such as a nearby park. Poses to consider:

- ❤ The bride alone, holding her bouquet

- ❤ The bride and groom together

- ❤ The bride and groom's hands, showing their wedding rings

- ❤ Bride and groom with the bride's parents

- ❤ Bride and groom with the bride's parents and siblings

- ❤ Bride and groom with the bride's parents, siblings, and grandparents

- ❤ Bride and groom with the groom's parents

- ❤ Bride and groom with the groom's parents and siblings

♥ Bride and groom with the groom's parents, siblings, and grandparents

♥ Bride and groom with both sets of parents

♥ Bride and groom with both sides of the family, parents, siblings, and grandparents

♥ Bride and groom with the maid of honor and the best man

♥ Bride and groom with their wedding party

Photographs Taken at Your Wedding Reception

Many of the photos from your reception will be candid shots; however, there are some specific moments you will not want your photographer to miss.

♥ Bride and groom getting out of the car at the reception

♥ Bride and groom entering the reception

♥ The receiving line

♥ The buffet table, if you have one

♥ The parents' table

♥ The bride and groom at the head table

♥ The wedding party at the head table

♥ The toast by the best man

♥ The cutting of the cake

♥ Bride and groom feeding each other a bite of cake

♥ The bride and groom's first dance as husband and wife

❤ The bride dancing with her father

❤ The groom dancing with his mother

❤ The tossing of the wedding bouquet

❤ The removal and the tossing of the garter

❤ Bride and groom with the people who caught the bouquet and the garter

❤ The bride and groom leaving the reception

You may have some other ideas for photographs you want. Be sure to discuss those with the photographer you hire.

What Are You Paying For?

Wedding photography is expensive. As already mentioned, the average cost in the United States for photography packages is $3,000. This price can dip or rise depending on where you live, what packages you choose, and the popularity of the photographer. The following explanations will help you make sense of "photographer speak" when you begin interviewing them.

❤ An exposure is the term used every single time the photographer clicks his or her camera. Typical weddings and receptions have about 150-200 exposures taken in total, throughout the day. A word of advice: Be cautious with any wedding photograph package that limits the amount of exposures. Also, if your photographer is using a digital camera instead of a film camera, this will not be an issue.

❤ A proof is not what it used to be. Before digital technology became the norm, photographers would print the pictures they shot into smaller sizes, and then display them in an album for you to choose from. Today, proofs are often handled by CD, via a computer. Some photographers will display your proofs in a slide show at their studio.

❤ Prints are simply the proofs you have chosen, enlarged into the final prints in the sizes you have selected. You will likely have a selection of 5x5 prints up to larger sizes, such as 8x10, 10x10, or 11x13. The more large prints you order, the more money it will cost. This is something to consider when looking over the different package prices a photographer offers. If you and your fiancé know you will want many of the larger-sized prints, pay close attention to the pricing to be sure the deal you are getting is what you actually want.

Finding the Right Photographer for Your Wedding

Good wedding photographers are not hard to come by; however, finding ones that fall into your budget may be. Also, different photographers have varying styles, so you will want one that falls into the vision you and your fiancé have for your wedding. When beginning the search for your wedding photographer, consider the following sources:

❤ Friends and family who have recently been married. This is a perfect way to find your photographer, because you will be able to view their photographs and ask about the photographer's pricing. It is one of the best methods to find the right photographer for you and your fiancé.

❤ Bridal shows are another great place to compare wedding photographers. There will likely be several at your local bridal show, with samples of their pictures and price lists in tow. This also gives you the ability to do quick interviews as you roam throughout the show.

❤ The Yellow Pages. Look under "photographers," but be sure you are selecting those who specialize in weddings. Many photographers will never place an ad in the Yellow Pages, but it is a good place to start if you are unable to find referrals from friends and family.

❤ Other wedding industry professionals you have hired. Ask your florist, your baker, your reception venue manager, and any other wedding professional for referrals.

❤ And of course, when you do select your photographer, be sure to keep a copy of the contract as well as any payment receipts. The contract should state all possible fees to the penny, so you are not taken unaware.

Questions to Ask Your Wedding Photographers

When you begin narrowing down the prospective photographers on your list, ask them these questions:

♥ What is the photographer's philosophy on wedding photography? You want to hear excitement in his or her voice — not boredom. You want to know that he or she is passionate about the work, because that will show in your photos.

♥ What is the photographer's preferred style of taking shots? This could be the traditional posed photographs, candid shots, portraits, or even photojournalism. Any photographer that makes it though this first round should be willing to show you examples, and those samples should match the answer — for the most part.

♥ Does the photographer shoot primarily in black and white, color, or both? If you have a preference, will he or she adhere to that?

♥ Does he or she shoot with film, digitally, or both? It may affect some of the final costs, as film costs more than digital.

♥ Be sure the photographer you talk to and meet with is the one you are actually hiring. If a different photographer shows up to your wedding, you may not get the pictures you thought you would. After all, photographers have different styles.

♥ How does the photographer work? Does he or she require or prefer you to describe your desires, or does the photographer prefer to work independently with free rein? Or a mix of both?

♥ How many weddings has the photographer done? What percentage of their business is made up of weddings? Photographers with limited experience at weddings may not give you the photos you need.

♥ Can you and your fiancé specify a list of must-take photos? This could be certain shots of you and your fiancé, a picture of the bride with her great-great grandmother, or anything else that is important to you.

♥ Will the photographer be shooting for any other wedding(s) on the same day as your wedding? It is best if his or her time is dedicated to your wedding.

♥ How is pricing determined? Is it by exposures, proofs, or prints — or a combination of all three? Or is it by the total number of hours the photographer works?

♥ Does the photographer have wedding picture packages available?

♥ Can you see a full price list?

♥ When does the photographer arrive at your wedding ceremony?

♥ How will you see your photos? Contact sheets, proofs, CD, video, a slide show in their studio, or via their Web site?

♥ What type of equipment and lighting does the photographer use? Is there backup equipment available in case of a problem?

♥ Will the photographer develop the film or does another person/ company to do that? How long are the negatives stored? Are you able to purchase the negatives?

♥ Can you see any references from past wedding clients?

What to Know — Hiring Your Photographer

These tips will assist you in choosing your photographer:

♥ Remember, you are not only after the best price. The quality of the photographs, the package deals, and the samples you view should all be a part of your end decision.

♥ Check credentials. In addition to speaking with past clients, find out if the photographers you are interested in are members of the Professional Photographer's Association of America. If they are, you can be sure they have been well trained. You can learn more at their Web site: **www.ppa.com**.

♥ Check in with the Better Business Bureau at **www.bbb.org**. Ask if any of the photographers on your list have had any complaints brought against them.

♥ When choosing between photographers, you may be tempted to go with a brand-new photographer because his or her prices are less expensive. However, do not forget that experience goes a long way in getting those special moments you will want to have forever on film. Look for photographers with a minimum of three to five years of experience.

♥ View their sample albums with a critical eye. Sure, the photos are going to be beautiful, but look beyond that. You want to see different types of lighting, settings, and more than the posed shots. It is the candid moments that will bring those special memories back.

♥ Trust your instincts. Are you comfortable with the photographer? Do you feel confident in his or her abilities? Rave reviews do not matter if you do not like the person.

Ways to Save — Your Wedding Photography

Wedding photography can cost a large amount of money. There are ways to save throughout the process, as well as other methods you can use to stick to your budget.

If you are hiring a professional wedding photographer, consider these tips:

♥ You do not have to hire a photographer for the entire time. Consider having a professional photographer at your ceremony and the first couple of hours at your reception to reduce costs.

♥ Or consider hiring the photographer for only the ceremony and using volunteer photographers made up of friends and family for the reception. More on this follows.

♥ How much time passes between your ceremony and reception? Minimize the time to no more than an hour so you are not paying "dead" time to the photographer. The exception to this is if the photographer wants to use that time to get some special shots of you, your fiancé, and the wedding party.

♥ Consider how many pictures you need before looking through the packages the photographer offers. Decide if you want to offer special albums to the wedding party and the parents. Decide how many you want for gifts to special friends and family members. Decide how many you want for your personal collection. When going through the packages, be firm and stick to your decision so you do not go overboard.

♥ If you do not see a package that fits your needs, ask about a custom package to get exactly what you and your fiancé want.

♥ Some photographers allow you to keep the proofs for free. If so, this is a great savings. You can take these proofs to have color copies made, or you can scan them into your computer and print them off on your own color photo printer.

♥ Wedding photograph albums are beautiful but can be pricey. Choose your album without extra decorations. Your pictures are all you need.

♥ Your formal wedding album does not have to be huge. Consider ordering a smaller album, one with 24 or 36 pages instead of 48. You will have plenty of other pictures to show your special day.

♥ If you have decided to order special wedding albums for your and your fiancé's parents, you do not have to order an overly large album. A smaller album, showcasing the most beautiful shots, will make your family members beam just as much as a larger album will.

♥ And, if you want to skip ordering special albums for your parents, grandparents, or wedding party — feel free to do so. It will be simple enough to make your own for far less cost. In addition, you can always ask your parents if they are interested in purchasing their own album from the professional photographer.

♥ If it is important to you and your fiancé to include the parents' albums in your photography budget, look for packages that offer them. This may save you money in the long run.

♥ Ask your photographer if black-and-white prints are less expensive than color prints. If they are, consider having a nice mix of color and black-and-white. Black-and-white photographs are classic, elegant, and can be breathtaking.

♥ Unless it is important to you and your fiancé, do not bother having the professional portraits taken before the wedding. These add extra dollars that, instead, could be used toward the wedding day photographs.

♥ Many photographers offer special printing of your photographs. These are gimmick shots, such as a picture of you and your fiancé superimposed over another picture. These are not necessary and will not do anything to add to your memories of your wedding.

♥ Along the same manner, do you need special borders, cropping, retouching, sepia or other types of tones, or any of the other little extras the photographer will offer? Each of these specialties will add up.

❤ Hire a photographer who works independently. Photographers with assistants are going to cost you more money — they have to pay their assistants.

If paying a professional photographer is simply out of your budget, no matter how you try to do it, you can ask for volunteers to help with the photo shooting. This is especially true if you have a friend or family member who is comfortable behind the camera and has plenty of experience taking pictures.

You can still receive beautiful photographs. Do not despair over this. If you are considering letting your friends and family volunteers snap your wedding photographs for you, consider these tips:

❤ One area you should not try to save on is film. Purchase high-quality film to receive high-quality photos.

❤ Visit bulk discount stores to stock up on high-quality film. Multipacks will offer you the biggest savings.

❤ Try to have more than one volunteer snapping pictures for you at your wedding ceremony and reception. Two or three is best, as they will be able to make up for their lack of experience by offering you a greater quantity of photos to choose from. Plus, they can each take breaks to enjoy the celebration if the responsibility is scattered.

❤ Give your volunteers a list of people, moments, and other photographs you want taken. Do not assume they will know you want a picture of the best man delivering his toast — tell them.

❤ When using volunteers, you want to be sure to cut out the possibility of not receiving the key moments on film. Have them take several shots of the major parts of your ceremony and reception to be sure bad lighting or a faulty flash does not ruin that one special shot you want.

❤ Buy throwaway cameras to put on all the guest tables. Guests can be a part of your photography crew, and this way, you will have an extremely large selection of precious moments to look at for a lifetime.

- ♥ Comparison shop heavily for picture developing. You may find better deals at a local store than you will online. Take your time to search for the best prices and the best quality.

- ♥ As tempted as you may be to use a one-hour shop for developing your wedding day pictures, do not go this route. One, it will cost you extra money, and two, chances are you will not have high-quality photos for the increased price.

- ♥ If you have a large number of rolls of film to develop, find out if you can arrange a bulk discount on developing. It never hurts to ask.

Online Sources — Wedding Photography

There are many sites on the Internet dedicated to photography, finding the right photographer, discount film, and more. These sites will give you more information on wedding photography:

- ♥ Craigs List — **www.craigslist.org**

- ♥ eCameraFilm — **http://ecamerafilms.stores.yahoo.net/corporatesales.html**

- ♥ Elegala.com — **www.elegala.com/lookforless-04.html**

- ♥ Event Pix — **www.eventpix.com**

- ♥ Photo Reflect — **www.photoreflect.com**

- ♥ Pictage — **www.pictage.com**

- ♥ Wedding and Portrait Photographers — **www.wppionline.com**

- ♥ Wedding Photography on a Budget — **www.associatedcontent.com/article/157956/how_to_get_wedding_photography_on_a.html**

- ♥ Wedding Photo USA — **www.weddingphotousa.com/disposableweddingcameras.htm**

- ♥ Wedding Photojournalist Association — **www.wpja.com**

If you want to post your pictures online, check out these sites:

♥   Kodak Easy Share Gallery — **www.kodakgallery.com**

♥   Photoworks — **www.photoworks.com**

♥   Shutterfly — **www.shutterfly.com**

CASE STUDY: MARK LAWLEY AND ASSOCIATES WEDDING PHOTOGRAPHY

What is your area of expertise?

Wedding photography.

What are the most common mistakes that result in the bride and groom going over budget?

Oddly, I've seen brides hire less than competent photographers, based on price alone, then have to spend many more dollars having someone else try to salvage enough to have wedding photographs they can display.

If you could offer one piece of advice to a couple planning their own wedding under a budget, what would it be?

Hire the best photographer you can afford. Prioritize your photography in the budget. Look for value rather than low price. This is an area you truly get what you pay for. Be sure to look at the quality of the photographer's work. Look for attention to details.

What are overlooked areas of savings?

Find a photographer who has good skills but uses budget-priced album companies. This cuts the final cost.

How do a bride and groom stay on budget?

Research! Know what is available in your area, and look a little farther from home. Sometimes brides can find high-quality photographers with lower prices a couple of hours' drive away. The lower pricing can offset travel fees and the result can be much higher quality photography at the same or lower cost than local photographers.

What is the biggest misconception you see in wedding planning?

In my own area of expertise, it is that all photographers are equal, that all provide the same level of service, and brides look for the most "stuff" for the least investment. All are not equal.

CASE STUDY: MARK LAWLEY AND ASSOCIATES
WEDDING PHOTOGRAPHY

How can a couple find quality services at the best price?

Research! Meet with potential photographers. Ask questions related to their services, quality, etc., not just price. Be certain that your expectations are conveyed prior to booking a photographer and that you are satisfied that the particular photographer can meet or exceed those expectations.

What shouldn't the bride and groom do to cut costs?

Find a friend with a good camera or even a friend who "takes great pictures" to photograph their wedding. These folks most often do not know how to deal with the fluid situations of a wedding. They may be able to take good landscape photos or even pretty good portraits under controlled situations, and still not be able to handle the pressures of a wedding. You get one shot at doing it right. Hire an experienced pro.

Do you have an example to share that shows how a bride and groom saved money?

There are many examples of people "saving money" on photography, but it often leads to disappointment with their photographs. Brides or grooms with experience in graphic design might hire a pro who will deliver the images to the bride and groom and design their own wedding album. Many brides and grooms have forgone a finished wedding album (to cut costs) and purchased a full set of smaller-sized prints.

It's easy to become overwhelmed when planning a wedding. What is your advice for lowering the stress?

Hire a wedding planner! !

How would a couple know when a price is truly "too good to be true"?

When the price quoted is drastically below the normal range of the market price for wedding photography. Example: If the range of starting prices for a full-time, working, professional wedding photographer is $3,000-5,000 in the area, then a price of $800 will probably lead to disappointment.

Any other suggestions or advice you would like to share?

Before developing the wedding photography budget, decide how many dollars will be allocated to each item. Do some research to see what prices actually are. With the range of pricing available, a reasonable, realistic budget can be developed.

CASE STUDY: MARK LAWLEY AND ASSOCIATES WEDDING PHOTOGRAPHY

Give serious priority to the items important to you. If your friends getting drunk is more important than quality photography, by all means, have an open bar and buy a few disposable cameras. If you are on a budget and you want quality photography that will enable you to relive your wedding long after the hangovers are forgotten, seriously consider not spending so much on alcohol or forgoing alcohol altogether.

It really is possible to have a nice wedding on a reasonable budget, but you have to do your homework. You have to make tough decisions and prioritize.

I realize this sounds self-serving, but photography and video are two areas where brides can go too far in trying to save money. These are areas where the result cannot be seen until after the wedding, and changes cannot be made then.

If she cuts back on flower costs, even doing them herself or having a friend do the arrangements, they can be manipulated until they are as she wants them.

Good cakes can be bought at large supercenters or chain grocery stores with delicatessens and cost much less than a custom cake maker.

Nice, elegant gowns can be purchased at discounts, online, or even second hand, saving thousands over designer gowns. If it isn't just like she wants it, a seamstress can make alterations.

To save on food costs, she can plan a 2 o'clock wedding or even have friends or family do the food prep and serving.

However, if she tries to cut too deeply into the photography or video budget, she will not realize a mistake has been made until it is too late.

Mark Lawley

Mark Lawley and Associates Wedding Photography

www.marklawleyphotography.com

mark@marklawleyphotography.com

Experience The Difference

✑ Final Thoughts ✑

Hiring a photographer will cost a fair chunk of your wedding budget, but a professional photographer, with the appropriate experience and training, will grab all those amazing moments of your wedding day and preserve them for a lifetime. You can save money and still have beautiful professional photographs by comparison shopping, looking closely at package prices, and being creative with your photographer.

Even if you cannot hire a professional photographer, you can still have the photographs you want for your wedding day. Family and friends will be happy to help you capture the day.

The goal, at the end, is to have the pictures you want to save, to display, and to give as gifts that will showcase your wedding ceremony and celebration in the best possible way.

Videography for Your Wedding Day

Capturing special moments on video is becoming a standard for weddings. After all, not only will it give you the sights of your wedding day, but the action, sounds, and ambience as well. If you and your fiancé have considered hiring a videographer for your wedding but are not sure of the ins and outs, what you need to know, and what it is going to cost, you are not alone. This section will clear up the mystery of videography and will help you and your fiancé decide if this is a route you want to take.

The average cost of hiring a videographer for your wedding hovers between $650-1,500, depending on your location, editing, music, and the amount of copies you want. This price can fluctuate to lower and much higher costs, especially if extras are purchased, so be careful when deciding which video package is right for your wedding.

Wedding Video — What Are You Purchasing?

When you decide to hire a video professional for your wedding, you are paying for their time and labor, their expertise, and for the end product. Here is a breakdown to familiarize yourself with the process:

The Videographer's Time and Labor

The biggest chunk of a videographer's fees will likely be in time and labor.

As you begin interviewing videographers and reviewing price lists, you will see that they charge for the amount of time they are at your wedding, with a time limit that spans anywhere from three to six hours. If you require a longer amount of time than the package price, you may be charged a fee for each additional hour.

In addition to paying for time, you are also paying for expertise, his or her personality, and ability to mix in with your guests to get the video you want. This is why you want to ascertain that any videographer you hire has a lively personality and is a comfortable person to be around.

The End Product — Your Video

Today, you are likely ordering a DVD of your wedding footage. However, there is much more to it than taking footage, putting it on the appropriate VHS tape or DVD, and passing it over to you. After all, if that is all you needed, you could ask for volunteers to take videos. You are looking for a combination of raw footage, edited footage, and highlights of your day. Here is a more in-depth look at these areas:

Raw Footage

Raw footage is exactly how it sounds. There is no interruption of the video; it is just a play-by-play video story of your wedding day. Although you can purchase a raw footage video, and it is the least-expensive option, you will likely not be happy with this. If you do decide you just want raw footage, with no editing and no special highlight section, you may want to consider asking volunteers to do this. Professional videographers will mix it up more and offer you a combination of raw footage plus other specialties.

Edited Footage

There are actually two types of editing that can be done with your video. In-camera editing is what happens when the videographer uses the camera during your ceremony and/or reception to edit out uninteresting sections of the video and then turns the camera back on to resume recording. You can hire videographers who will do no post editing work at all but will use in-camera editing to help fine tune your video throughout your wedding.

Post editing is the most common type of editing that occurs. In this case, the videographer will go through the recording after the ceremony and reception and make edits by cutting out boring sections; smoothing transitions; and even adding in titles, music, and other specialties.

Highlights on Your Wedding Video

Highlights are a great option that many professional videographers offer to their clients. Think of it as a movie preview. The videographer will use titles and music to put together a 10- to 15-minute highlight video of your entire wedding day. You will still receive the full video, but in addition, you will get a capsule of your day to share with people who may not want to sit through several hours of video.

Copies of Your Wedding Video

Although you will likely receive one copy of your wedding day video as part of your package price, you may want to purchase extra copies for the wedding party, your parents, and maybe far-away friends and family who were unable to attend the wedding. Each copy will add money on to your final tally.

Wedding Video — What Do You Want?

When planning what parts of your ceremony and reception you want covered in your wedding video, take a look at the list of "must-have" wedding photographs you have put together. These are likely the same shots you will want to have in your wedding video. In addition, some sentimental moments you may want to catch on video are:

- ♥ You and/or your fiancé's grandparents dancing at the reception.

- ♥ You and/or your fiancé's parents dancing at the reception.

❤ Friends and/or family with their new baby and children — especially if they live far away.

❤ If you know someone is going to propose at your reception, get that on tape. The happy couple will thank you.

❤ Any other special moments you know about ahead of time. A great-aunt's birthday, a cousin who is joining the armed forces and is being sent overseas, a crazy dance, or presentations the groomsmen are doing are all examples of this.

Finding the Right Videographer for Your Wedding

Good wedding videographers are not as easily found as photographers; however, they are out there. Different videographers will likely have varying styles, so you will want one that falls into the vision you and your fiancé have for your wedding. When beginning the search for your wedding videographer, consider the following sources:

❤ Friends and family who have recently been married. If they hired a videographer, ask to see their wedding video and the dollar amount the videographer charged. Take an evening or two and view the videos. What do you like? Are there things you do not like? Take notes.

❤ Bridal shows are a terrific place to scout out potential videographers. There will likely be several at your local bridal show, with samples of their videos and price lists in tow. You can also take some time interviewing them.

❤ The Yellow Pages. Look under "video production services."

❤ There are professional associations to help you find a qualified videographer in your area. Check out The Wedding and Event Videographers at **www.weva.com**. You can also go to Videomasters at **www.videomasters.net**.

❤ Other wedding industry professionals you have hired, especially your photographer. But you should also ask your florist, your baker, your reception venue manager, and any other wedding professionals for referrals.

♥ Television stations are a possibility. Many times there are professional camera operators who moonlight by shooting weddings. The benefit is that they will likely have a high-quality camera and will have the experience to grab those candid moments as they happen. If you call, ask to speak to a camera person directly, or leave a message.

♥ And of course, when you do select your videographer, be sure to keep a copy of the contract, as well as any payment receipts. All possible fees should be included on the contract.

Questions to Ask Wedding Videographers

When you have acquired a list of possible videographers and you need to begin narrowing down names, ask the following questions:

♥ Do they have a style they tend to use? Make sure their style measures up to your vision.

♥ How many weddings have they recorded?

♥ What is the approach they take to capturing your wedding on video?

♥ Has the videographer worked with your photographer in the past? Do they have a good working relationship? It is important that these two professionals communicate, so be sure to find out.

♥ Have they worked at your ceremony and reception venue in the past? Was it for a wedding, a bar mitzvah, or another type of event? Do they know the locale well enough to plan their method ahead of time?

♥ If the answers to the above questions are yes, can you view the tape? This will give you an excellent clue as to how they work.

♥ Do they have any other planned events on the same day as your wedding? You want to ascertain that there are no time constraints.

♥ Can you see a full price list and different packages the videographer offers?

♥ Be sure the videographer you are interviewing is the one who will be at your wedding. Your goal in interviewing is to find the right match, so if another person shows up — one you have never met or spoken with — you may not receive the end product you thought you would.

♥ What type of equipment does the videographer use? Is it high quality? How old is the equipment? Are there backups if necessary, and will they be on hand?

♥ If you are considering an edited video, ask about the equipment the video will be edited on. Digital video-editing equipment typically produces the highest quality of video.

♥ How many people are in the video crew? Will they be dressed professionally? Can you meet them before your wedding?

♥ Is the video shooting style of the videographer obtrusive? How bright will the lights be?

♥ Do they insist on being paid the full amount up front? Try to avoid this. You should be able to find a professional videographer who will accept a deposit, with the final amount due on delivery of product.

♥ Can you have a list of references?

♥ Can you view other wedding videos the videographer has shot?

What to Know — Hiring Your Videographer

After you have narrowed your list of videographers down, these tips will assist you in choosing your videographer:

♥ Remember, you are not only after the best price. The quality of the video, the package deals, and the expertise of the videographer are all important aspects of the decision you are making.

♥ When viewing the sample videos, you want to pay attention to several different aspects. Is the video in focus? Are the transitions smooth? How does it sound?

♥ Check in with the Better Business Bureau at **www.bbb.org**. Ask if any of the videographers on your list have had any complaints brought against them.

♥ Consider experience. Although less experienced videographers may charge less money, you may end up with a choppy, unprofessional video. Look for videographers with a minimum of two years of experience. On the other hand, if you like the work of a videographer who is new to the business and the price is right — go with your instincts.

♥ Trust your instincts. Are you comfortable with the videographer? Do you feel confident in his or her abilities? Rave reviews do not matter if you do not like them.

Ways to Save — Your Wedding Video

Your video can cost several hundred dollars or several thousand dollars, depending on the experience and expertise of the videographer, the type of product you want, and the number of copies you decide to purchase. You can save money, though; the following tips will give you some ideas if you are hiring a professional videographer:

♥ Comparison shop widely. Do not hire the first videographer you like; continue through your list so you can be sure you are hiring the highest quality you can afford.

♥ Three-chip cameras are not a necessity. A standard VHS camera will get the job done and be more cost effective.

♥ If your videographer has experience with in-camera editing, have him or her do as much of that as possible during the ceremony and reception. You will save money later, because the post edit work will not take as long.

♥ Forgo the post edit work altogether. If your videographer has the experience to completely edit in camera, you will save money.

♥ Forget about the special effects if you are on a tight budget. You do not need fancy editing and special effects to have a wedding video you will love. In fact, too many extras will only detract from the images captured. Keep it simple and save.

♥ If your videographer gives you the offer of having two cameras set up in different areas, skip it. The extra camera will cost more money, and you end up paying for twice the manpower, twice the time, and twice the editing.

♥ When considering the various packages, if there is not one that is right for you, do not overspend. Instead, ask the videographer if a custom package can be built for you.

♥ Consider hiring a professional videographer to record your wedding ceremony only, and ask for volunteers among your family and friends to record the reception.

♥ If your wedding date is during a less popular wedding month, try to negotiate an off-season discount.

♥ If you and your fiancé decide you want to order several copies of the wedding video, ask about a bulk discount.

♥ Instead of having the videographer make the copies, make them yourself.

♥ If you live in a big city, scout around in the smaller neighboring towns. You may find less expensive fees.

❤ Call your local university or college and ask if it has a film or media studies department. If so, consider hiring a student.

❤ Some videographers are now offering HD video. This option will cost you a large increase, so skip it.

If your wedding budget simply cannot stretch wide enough to fit in a professional videographer but you have your heart set on a wedding day video, consider asking a friend or family member to help out with the video instead. In fact, you may want to see if you can get several volunteers to help. If this is the route you decide to go, consider these helpful hints:

❤ With more than one video volunteer, you can get different angles. This is a good choice when not using a professional, as you will have a better chance of getting all the moments captured that you want.

❤ When purchasing the tapes for your volunteers, resist the temptation to buy too many. Instead, select tapes that are longer-running. Not only will this save you money, but you will have less missed time.

❤ You will likely need to have your volunteer videos edited. Try to arrange this ahead of time or see if any of your friends or family members have experience with editing tapes. It is not as difficult as it sounds to have an end product that is well edited.

❤ Make sure to label the tapes appropriately during the ceremony so a recorded tape is not used twice. You could buy two colors of stickers. Red can be for tapes that have already been recorded on and green for those that are empty.

❤ Because you will be using volunteers, make sure they know what you want captured on film. You could write up a list to give them so they do not miss any of the moments you want.

Online Sources — Videography

Whether you want more information on hiring a professional videographer or you want ideas on the video itself, the following Web sites will answer many of your questions:

- ❤ Advice for Wedding Videographers — **www.bealecorner.com/ trv900/wedding.html**

- ❤ Bridal Tips — **www.bridaltips.com/video.htm**

- ❤ Videomaker — **www.videomaker.com/article/8983**

- ❤ Wedding Bee — **www.weddingbee.com/2007/05/08/why-hire-a- videographer**

- ❤ Wedding How To — **www.weddinghowto.com/videographer.htm**

- ❤ Wedding Video Package Advice and Tips — **www.gavinholt.com/ packageadvice.html**

Final Thoughts

Having a wedding video is a personal choice. It is not right for everyone, but if you and your fiancé have decided you definitely want a wedding video, you do not have to spend a large sum of money to get a great product. Get as many referrals as you can, do your homework, compare prices, packages, and quality, and be firm in what your vision is. The wedding videographer you hire should be able to match his/her style with your vision.

Even if you cannot hire a professional videographer and have to go the route of volunteers, you can still have a video you will be proud of, one you will watch many times as the years pass. That is your final goal, after all.

The Wedding Web Site

Many couples today choose to put their wedding photographs online on their own personal Web site. This is a great way to share photos without purchasing extras for a lot of people, not to mention for people who were unable to attend. It is also a terrific method for building excitement before the wedding arrives if it is used as a planning site for the wedding party, guests, and even the industry professionals you have hired.

Your wedding Web site should be a style that suits you and your fiancé. It should reflect your combined vision, love, and commitment to each other. In fact, a wedding Web site is another form of celebration — one that all of your friends and family can take part in.

Technology today means you can have a wedding Web site for little cost. In fact, you may be able to make your site for free.

The following online sources are chock-full of information you can use if you decide to put together a wedding Web site:

❤ eWedding.com — **www.ewedding.com**

❤ My Event.com — **www.myevent.com**

❤ Onewed.com — **www.onewed.com/articles/wedding_article_56.html**

❤ Wed Share.com — **www.wedshare.com**

❤ Wedding Announcer.com — **www.weddingannouncer.com**

❤ Weddings USA — **www.weddingusa.com/stories/website.shtml**

✍ Final Thoughts ≋

Wedding Web sites can be a lot of fun, an efficient way to share information, and a special place for loved ones to view every detail of your wedding — from the planning of it to the big day itself. You can make a wedding Web site for little money, if any, and the results are well worth it.

Little Extras That Mean A Lot

Often, it is the little extras that add the most to a wedding day. The ride in the limo, the guest favors, or the special gifts purchased for the wedding party can all leave an impression that lasts far beyond the actual wedding day. This chapter focuses on these extras.

Transportation for Your Wedding Day

Some brides want a limousine, others want something more unique, and for some the way they arrive at their wedding is not important, as long as they are there on time. Whether you already have your transportation in mind or are still unsure if you want a limousine or another form of transportation, you can arrive at your wedding in style.

Limousines for Your Wedding Day Transportation

Renting a limousine is the most popular choice for weddings and for good reason. Limos are sleek, stylish, and elegant. If a limousine fits into your budget, you will find it a perfect way to get to the church on time.

Regular limousines can carry one to three people comfortably, and stretch limos are great for larger groups, up to ten. Some limousine companies offer limo Hummers and/or vans for extra large numbers of passengers. Therefore, before you begin shopping around, you will want to decide how many limousines you want to rent and how many passengers will be in each one.

Limousines offer a varied selection of amenities, some of which are:

♥ A Professional Chauffeur

♥ TV, VCR, DVD Player, and/or a Stereo

♥ Cell Phone

♥ Lighted Bar

♥ Leather Seating

♥ Hot Tub

♥ Sun Roofs

Limousine rentals can be from $50 to several hundred dollars per hour, depending on your needs and the type of limo you rent. The vehicle and driver make up the cost.

First, you are paying for the limousine and the amenities. The more luxurious the model, the more expensive the price tag. If you choose a stretch limo, it is important to realize it can come in different sizes. Be sure to ask how many the limousine will comfortably seat.

You are also paying for the professional driver. He or she will be dressed appropriately and will act in a professional manner. So, your limousine rental fee covers the chauffer's time and demeanor as well.

How To Find a Reliable Limousine Service

If you have decided to go with a limousine, or more, on your wedding day, you want to find the right service. Here are some tips for sources:

♥ Ask for referrals from family and friends who have recently been married.

♥ Check with the other wedding industry professionals you have hired to get their opinions.

♥ Your Yellow Pages. Look up "limousines."

Questions to Ask the Limousine Services

Ask the following questions to any limousine services you are considering:

♥ What limousine types and sizes are available? How many people can comfortably fit into each type and size?

♥ What amenities are included with the price, and which cost extra?

♥ Do they offer a wedding discount package? For limousine rental companies that do, you may get a free bottle of champagne or another congratulatory gift.

♥ Are they a member of the National Limousine Association? Check them out at **www.limo.org**.

♥ If you need more than one limousine, will you receive a discount for each additional rental?

♥ Does the fee come with a set amount of miles and gas, or is that an extra fee?

♥ What will the driver wear? Unless your wedding is ultra casual, you do not want the chauffer showing up in jeans and a T-shirt.

8. Are you able to review their operating license and insurance certificate?

Ways to Save — Renting a Limousine

The following tips may help you cut costs on renting a limousine:

♥ Forget the amenities if you have to pay extra for them. You will not be in the limo long enough to make the fullest use of them.

♥ If you need to rent multiple cars, rent one limousine, for the bride and groom only. Rent other types of vehicles for the wedding party and visiting family and friends.

♥ Avoid limousine companies that have a three- or four-hour minimum time requirement, unless you need one for that long. Most wedding couples require a limo for two hours or less.

♥ If your wedding is on an off night, you will save money with a limo service. Peak nights are Friday and Saturday, so transportation for a Sunday wedding should cost less.

♥ Hire a corporate limousine company, if possible. Companies that specialize in renting limos to executives tend to charge less.

♥ Compare packages and prices. You may be surprised at the difference between two companies with a nearly identical package.

♥ If you are renting a limousine for only you and your fiancé, choose a regular limo instead of a stretch limo. The look will be just as jazzy, but the price will be more reasonable.

♥ Color matters. For some reason, white limousines cost more to rent than black ones do.

♥ Take a chance and ask about "free" extras. Many limo companies now offer free amenities such as a red carpet leading to the door, a bottle of champagne, and even snacks stocked in the limo. Some of them do not offer these unless asked, however.

♥ Watch your time. Do whatever you can to not have the limo stand by, idly waiting for a long period of time. This will add to your final cost in a big way.

Online Sources — Limousines for Your Wedding

The following Web sites offer more information on renting a limousine for your wedding:

♥ Limos.com — **www.limos.com/content/wedding_limo_rental_ planning.aspx**

♥ WedAlert.com — **www.wedalert.com/content/articles/Renting_ a_Limo.asp**

♥ Wedding Solutions.com — **www.weddingsolutions.com/ Wedding_Limousines.htm**

Other Types of Wedding Transportation

Your transportation does not have to be a limousine. If your wedding calls for a different type of transportation, use your imagination to match your style and your vision. Here are some possible ideas:

♥ Horse and carriage is a popular and romantic choice. All Wedding Companies — **www.allweddingcompanies.com/carriages/index. html** — offers a search to find horse and carriage transportation in many locales.

♥ Antique cars are another fantastic choice. Although there are professional antique car rental companies, you could also try calling a local antique car collectors' club for referrals.

♥ Rent a sedan. They are beautiful and cost less than a limousine.

♥ If you and your fiancé having a casual, fun wedding, consider a motorcycle for two.

♥ If you have a friend with a sporty convertible or a fancy foreign car, find out if he or she would be willing to play chauffer to you and your fiancé.

♥ Or simply catch a ride from your parents and save more money.

Final Thoughts

There is no wrong choice in transportation for your wedding. Select a mode that fits your style, your budget, and makes you and your fiancé happy. Do not stress over such a small portion of your wedding day. Your wedding day will be filled with magical moments that are far more important than the type of transportation you use.

Gifts for Your Wedding Party

Purchasing gifts for your wedding party is a long-standing tradition. The gifts you choose should reflect your style and vision of your wedding, and they should be chosen with care. The reason for purchasing the gifts is to thank those friends and family who are in your wedding party or have contributed in some other way and, therefore, are a special addition to your wedding day.

Depending on the gifts you choose to purchase, and how many people you decide to buy gifts for, the cost can be minimal or it can be pricey. Consider the following when making gift-giving decisions:

GIFT IDEAS FOR THE WEDDING PARTY

Parents of the Bride and Groom	They may be given a gift in appreciation for their help in the planning and/or their financial contributions to your wedding, as well as to symbolize the family ties.
	Gift ideas: a wedding album, a framed wedding picture, a retouched photograph of their wedding day, an engraved bowl or vase, or a special memento that is unique to the parents.
Maid of Honor and Bridal Attendants	They traditionally are given a gift to thank them for their friendship, their help in planning your wedding, and for standing with you on your wedding day. The maid of honor's gift is often one of greater value than the other attendants, but this is not necessary.
	Gift ideas: bud vases, engraved photo frames, a wedding album, bath oils, gift certificates to a spa, key chains, a nice bottle of wine, or jewelry.
Best Man, Ushers, and Groomsmen	They are also traditionally given gifts as appreciation for their friendship and help with the wedding. The best man's gift is often of greater value than the groomsmen and ushers, but this is not necessary.
	Gift ideas: desk clocks, watches, business-card holders, engraved photo frames, key chains, pen and pencil sets, or a nice bottle of wine.
Flower Girls and Ring Bearers	They are young and excited to be a part of your wedding day. They should be given a gift to thank them for participating.
	Gift ideas: a framed picture of the married couple with the child, a favorite collectible of the child's, a stuffed animal, or other special toy.
Friends and Family who have Helped	They deserve a gift of appreciation and thanks. If your cousin has a beautiful voice and is singing at your ceremony, if your brother is volunteering to chauffer out-of-town guests to the ceremony and reception, or if any other special role is filled in a volunteer fashion, do not forget these important members of your wedding.
	Gift ideas: a framed photo, a gift certificate to a favorite restaurant, or a nice bottle of wine.

Other Considerations When Purchasing Gifts

If your wedding consists of a large wedding party, it may be a good idea to choose only two gifts — one for the men and a different one for the women. This will assist you in the costs, as you will likely be able to get a bulk discount. It will also save you time. Pens, clocks, key chains, and photo frames are all great ideas for this.

On the other hand, if your wedding is small and you have to purchase only a few gifts, you can spend a little more time focusing on individual gifts for people. If your fiancé's best man is an avid golfer, find him something golf related. If your maid of honor is a coffee addict, purchase gourmet coffee.

When you have a tight wedding budget to work with, it can be overwhelming to find quality gifts that will truly express your appreciation that fall within your budget. Do not despair. It can be done, and the following money-saving tips will get you started:

❤ Avoid the overpriced thank you gifts you see in bridal salons and catalogs. You can find better-priced items of equal, or higher, quality, elsewhere.

❤ Keep your eye on local stores and when they have sales. Check the newspaper for advertisements.

❤ Purchase in bulk. Whether pens, picture frames, or key chains, get them all at once, and you will likely save money.

❤ Gift certificates are always appreciated. This is a perfect way to stay in your budget. Whether you can spend $25, $50, $100, or more, purchase individual gift certificates in that amount. Some ideas are makeovers, manicures, music, restaurants, and hardware stores.

❤ If you are giving gifts to out-of-town friends and family that are staying in a hotel, arrange to have gift baskets with their favorite munchies delivered to them.

❤ Gift catalogs are a shopper's delight. **Catalogs.com** has plenty to choose from, and they will be sent to your door.

❤ Shop the Internet for great savings. Do a search and see how many venues pop up.

❤ The simplest gift will have more meaning if given with a heartfelt letter written by you and your fiancé.

Online Sources — Wedding Gifts

The following Web sites will give you more ideas for wedding gifts:

❤ American Bridal — **www.americanbridal.com/gifts.html**

❤ Beau Coup — **www.beau-coup.com/bridal-party-gifts.htm**

❤ The Rosemary Company — **www.rosemarycompany.com**

❤ A Special Gift — **www.aspecialgift.com**

❤ Things Remembered — **www.thingsremembered.com**

❤ Wedding Accessories — **www.weddingaccessories.net/attendan.htm**

Final Thoughts

Giving gifts to those who have helped make your special day even more memorable is an important tradition, but it does not have to take you over budget. Comparison shop, be creative, and spend wisely. You will be able to find the right choice for those you wish to show appreciation to, and you can stick to your wedding budget at the same time.

Wedding Memorabilia, Mementos, and Guest Favors

Guest favors for your wedding are a great way to thank your wedding guests for being a part of your day. These mementos can be extravagant and pricey, or they can be simple and budget-minded. The cost does not matter to your guests; they will appreciate the sentiment and the memory they can take home with them.

This is another area where you can be as creative as you want. It truly does not matter what your budget is; you can find the perfect wedding memorabilia for the right price.

A traditional guest favor of sugar-coated almonds wrapped in tulle does not have to cost a large amount of money, for example. Plus, the sugar-coated almonds traditionally symbolize the bitterness and the sweetness of marriage. If this thought does not appeal to you, there are many other possibilities. Here are a few:

❤ Small picture frames with a shot of you and your fiancé could be set at each place setting.

❤ Candles in a simple candle holder can be given to each guest.

❤ Wine stoppers, cocktail shakers, engraved books of matches, and key chains are also great ideas.

❤ Small vases with a single flower for each guest.

❤ Personalized anything. Mint tins, gift books, and ornaments are all modestly priced possibilities.

❤ Chocolates in personalized candy boxes.

❤ Wine bottles with personalized labels, while pricey, are a fun memento.

❤ Tea light candles in a personalized tin.

❤ Magnets

❤ Chopsticks

You can also combine two inexpensive favors, one being edible or consumable — such as matches or chocolate — and the other being a memento to save, such as a magnet or bookmark. There are so many possibilities, it would be impossible to list them all. The only limit is your imagination.

Ways to Save — Guest Favors

There are plenty of ways to save money on your wedding favors. Here are a few:

♥ Comparison shop to find what you want at the price you want. Prices will vary widely from one vendor to another.

♥ Purchase in bulk. For example, if you were purchasing engraved matches as guest favors and you will need 150, order them all from the same place to save the most amount of money. At Wedding Reception Ideas.com, the price barely changes from 50 matchbooks to 100. Check at **www.myweddingreceptionideas.com/30_strike_matchbook_wedding_favors.asp,** and you will see you can purchase 50 matchbooks for $29, 100 matchbooks for only $2 more at $31, and 150 for $46.

♥ If you see something you like at a bridal salon, do not buy it. Instead, jump on the Internet and do a search for that item. Chances are you will find it for significantly less money.

♥ Purchase slightly more than the amount of guests you have invited, but not too much more. You want enough extra in case more people show up than you have anticipated, but you do not need an extra 100 key chains lying around.

Online Sources — Wedding Favors

You will find some of the best deals on the Internet. Here are a few places to check out:

♥ Forever & Always — **www.foreverandalways.com**

- ❤ Forever Wed.com — **www.foreverwed.com**

- ❤ My Wedding Favors.com — **www.myweddingfavors.com**

- ❤ Oriental Trading Company — **www.orientaltrading.com**

- ❤ Wedding Things.com — **www.weddingthings.com**

- ❤ Wholesale Favors — **www.wholesalefavors.com**

∂*Final Thoughts*

Wedding favors are meant to be fun for you and your guests. They should be a way to thank your guests and to give them something to remember your wedding day with. You do not have to break your wedding budget to fulfill this wish. By being creative, comparison shopping, and focusing on simple rather than extravagant, you can find the guest favors you want at a price you can afford.

Conclusion

Your wedding day is one of the most special events of your lifetime. Not only do you want it to be magical, but you need it to fit realistically into the wedding budget you and your fiancé have created. This is not an impossible dream.

Things to Remember

When planning any large event, but most especially a wedding, it is essential to give yourself plenty of time. One of the keys to saving money is to give yourself ample time to comparison shop, find sales, work out discounts, and to keep the entire process as low stress as possible. If you can, give yourself a year to plan your wedding, as that is optimum for not only getting the best deals, but in also finding the best wedding ceremony location, reception venue, wedding gown, and all the other details that you will need to focus on.

Even if you do not have much time until your wedding, you can still find ways to cut costs and stick to your budget. You will not be able to be as flexible in certain areas, but you can be successful.

Organize and Keep Records

Organize well before you begin, and keep the process up throughout the entire planning period. Keep copies of all your contacts, contracts, agreements, checks, and payment receipts. Read the fine print before you sign any contract, and be absolutely sure there are no hidden fees.

If a problem occurs in any aspect of your wedding, you will have the paperwork to back you up. This will be essential in clearing up any mistakes that may happen, and it will save you many hours of stress and anxiety.

Let Your Creativity Fly

Your wedding is a reflection of you and your fiancé, so do not hesitate to be creative in any part of the process. Love is magic. Your wedding is magic. One of the great things in planning your own wedding is the freedom to be as creative as you want.

Creativity is also a great method in saving money. If you see decorations in a wedding magazine you love but cannot afford to do it "their" way, create your own way that fits into your budget using less expensive materials, flowers, lights, and/or candles. Open your mind.

There Is Always a Bargain

In every area of your wedding you can save money. Sometimes you will find the money-saving idea immediately. Other times you will have to work a bit harder to locate the bargains — but they are there. At the end of it, you will have a breathtaking wedding, without breaking your budget.

Good luck! Have fun! You have earned it!

Resources

- ❤ About.com — **www.about.com**

- ❤ Brides.com — **www.brides.com**

- ❤ Brittney Rays Bridal Florist — **www.brittneyrays.com**

- ❤ Cheap Chic Weddings.com — **www.cheap-chic-weddings.com**

- ❤ eHow.com, How To Do Just About Everything — **www.ehow.com**

- ❤ Fields, Denise and Alan. *"New & Improved!" Bridal Bargains,* Windsor Peak Press, 2007.

- ❤ How Stuff Works, Money Channel — **http://money.howstuffworks. com**

- ❤ iVillage, Budget — **http://home.ivillage.com/entertaining/ weddings/topics/0,,6rnqf17v,00.html**

- ❤ Naylor, Sharon. *1001 Ways to Save Money and Still Have a Dazzling Wedding,* McGraw-Hill, New York, 2002.

♥ Our Marriage.com — **http://ourmarriage.com**

♥ Roney, Carley and the editors of *The Knot*. *The Knot Ultimate Wedding Planner*, Broadway Books, New York, 1999.

♥ Stylish Wedding Ideas, Just Perfect — **http://stylishweddingideas.com**

♥ Warner, Diane. *How To Have A Big Wedding On A Small Budget*, Better Way Books, 1997.

♥ Wed Alert.com — **www.wedalert.com**

♥ Wedding Channel.com — **www.weddingchannel.com**

♥ Wedding Strategies.com — **www.weddingstrategies.com**

♥ The Wedding Wizards, Bridal Party Roles — **http://wedding-roles.theweddingwizards.com/the-parents-of-the-bride/?action=print**

♥ Wilson, Jan and Beth Wilson Hickman. *How To Have An Elegant Wedding For $5,000 Or Less*, Three Rivers Press, 1998.

Author Biography

Tracy Leigh is a successful freelance writer and the author of many bridal planning articles. Her first taste of planning a wedding on a budget was her own, and although it turned out terrific, she learned from her mistakes. Since then, she has gone on to help friends plan their own weddings in creative and budget-minded ways. She resides in her home state of Ohio, along with her husband and four children. Tracy is an officer in a community writing organization, reads constantly, and enjoys planning family gatherings. She can be reached at **Tracy@TracyLeighWrites.com.**

Index

A

Alcohol 22, 46, 77, 198, 199, 205, 206, 207, 208, 209, 211, 212, 257
Announcement 32, 238
Attendant 53, 55, 126, 184, 243
Attire 14, 18, 21, 34, 42-44, 49, 55, 83, 98, 121, 123, 126, 130, 134, 136

B

Best man 21, 31, 32, 50, 52, 54, 55, 58, 60-63, 196, 243, 245, 253, 275, 276
Bride 14, 20-22, 34, 35, 37, 42-44, 49, 51, 52, 58, 60, 62, 83, 86-88, 90, 91, 95, 96, 103, 109-111, 114, 129, 136, 157, 161, 162, 167, 168, 172, 181-183, 188, 190, 238, 239-246, 249, 255, 256, 272
Budget 14-19, 22-25, 30, 33-36, 39, 40, 41, 46, 55, 59, 60, 62-65, 68, 74, 76, 77, 82, 86, 87, 92, 98-100, 103-105, 108-110, 113, 121-123, 127-129, 141-143, 156, 157, 165, 167-169, 171, 176, 177, 178, 180-183, 188, 189, 194, 197, 198, 205-207, 211-214, 223, 225, 227, 232, 235, 238-241, 247, 251-253, 255-257, 265, 266, 270, 274, 276-278, 280-282

C

Cake 13, 14, 20, 26, 30, 41, 44, 47, 158, 176, 180, 184-196, 198, 199, 204, 205, 215, 219, 238, 241, 245, 257
Candles 56, 72, 169, 170-172, 175, 177, 178, 179, 180, 278, 282
Ceremony 13-15, 17, 18, 20, 21, 25, 29, 30-33, 39, 43-76, 78-83, 89, 92, 98, 99, 101, 110, 112, 113, 116, 119, 120, 125, 132, 135, 137, 139, 140, 141, 144, 145, 153-155, 157, 162-167, 169-174, 176, 179, 180, 188, 197, 200, 201, 223, 225-227, 230, 234, 235, 243, 244, 249, 251, 253, 258-260, 262, 265, 266, 275, 281
Children 57, 132, 133, 140, 146, 237, 261

D

Dancing 13, 50, 52, 100, 112, 118, 218, 246, 260

Decorations 26, 30, 31, 52, 66, 78, 161, 164, 167, 169, 170, 172-174, 176, 181, 187, 194, 196, 241, 251, 282

Duties 31, 49, 51, 52, 54, 57, 209

E

Entertainment 30, 213, 214, 221-223

F

Fees 20, 25, 28, 34, 45, 46, 61, 66, 68, 71, 72, 74, 76, 77, 82, 108, 163, 202, 206, 208, 209, 221, 222, 228, 234, 248, 255, 259, 262, 265, 282

Flower girl 31, 51, 133, 134, 157, 167, 244

Flowers 14, 15, 18, 19, 31, 34, 43, 44, 72, 86, 111, 113, 131, 133, 157-177, 180, 184, 187-189, 193, 194, 200, 241, 282

G

Gifts 14, 31, 32, 49, 51, 52, 55, 175, 184, 251, 258, 269, 274, 275-277

Groom 13, 20-22, 34, 35, 42-44, 49, 51, 52, 57-59, 63, 86, 87, 110, 116, 136, 137, 139, 157, 181-183, 185, 188, 190, 196, 238-240, 243-246, 255, 256, 272

Guests 18, 22, 24, 27, 29, 32, 37, 39-43, 47, 48, 50, 52, 53, 56, 57, 60, 70, 71, 78, 80, 81, 105, 136, 141, 144, 153, 169, 171, 173-175, 177, 183-186, 188-190, 198, 199, 205, 207-211, 214, 216, 218, 219, 222, 223, 226, 227, 230, 231, 243, 259, 268, 275, 277, 278-280

I

Invitations 14, 20, 31, 34, 42, 49, 50, 51, 52, 86, 141-153, 155, 156, 181, 184, 208

M

Maid of Honor 32, 50, 52, 54, 55, 58, 59, 126, 162, 242, 245, 275, 276

Music 13, 14, 25, 26, 30, 31, 43, 78, 81, 154, 213, 214, 216-219, 221, 222, 240, 258, 260, 276

P

Parents 13, 30, 31, 32, 39-41, 52, 58, 60, 61, 63-65, 125, 132, 133, 139, 238, 243-245, 251, 252, 260, 274, 275

Party 14, 15, 20, 21, 29, 30, 32, 42-44, 49-60, 62-64, 81, 83, 98, 125-133, 136, 138-140, 153, 154, 157, 167, 170, 181, 184, 189, 197, 200, 210, 212, 215, 218, 228-231, 233, 235, 238, 242, 245, 251, 252, 260, 268, 269, 272, 274, 276, 277

Photographer 30-32, 35, 36, 86, 237-241, 245- 258, 262

Program 26, 150, 153, 154, 155, 168

R

Receipts 28, 82, 108, 147, 183, 248, 262, 282

Rental 31, 46, 52, 60, 71, 73, 76, 86, 103, 138, 139, 140, 164, 173, 181, 228-235, 270, 271, 273

Ring 20, 31, 49-53, 73, 139, 140, 157, 244

Ring bearer 31, 51, 73, 139, 140, 157, 244

T

Travel 50, 55, 63, 67, 102, 255

U

Usher 59, 61, 62, 63

V

Vows 17, 31, 49, 50, 65, 68, 173, 174, 244